THE RAIL BIRD HUNTER'S BIBLE

JOE GUIDE

Virtualbookworm.com Publishing

"**The Rail Bird Hunters Bible**" Copyright 2014, by Walter (Joe Guide) Dinkins.
All rights reserved

No part of this book may be produced, stored in a retrieval system, or transmitted through any means: (electronic or written) - without the "express and written permission" of the author. All photos are by the author, except where noted, and all photos in the RAIL BIRD HUNTERS BIBLE are used by the author freely with the permission the photographer for that purpose.

ISBN: 978-1-62137-452-7
Library of Congress Control Number: 2014902786

JOE GUIDE OUTFITTERS ™

(www.joeguideoutfitters.com)
c/o PO Box # 11403
Wilmington, North Carolina 28404-1403

Please Note: "*Joe Guide*" and "*Joe Guide Outfitters*" are registered trademarks **TM**- *created and owned by Mr. Walter M. Dinkins of Wilmington, N.C., ESQ. He is also the Founder and CFO of* (**JOE GUIDE OUTFITTERS**)

Illustrations
Nikki Marie Dinkins

Photographs:
Darryl Bogart
R. Shawn Bennett
Bob White
Joe Guide
AZ1 Phillip Hanvey USN (Ret)
Jamie P. Hand
Doug Hisesditt
Scott Loudermilk
Dr. Philip Metz, M.D., USNR MC (Ret)
Major Ben Moise' DNR-Wildlife Division (Ret)
CDR Ray Moses, U.S.N. (Ret)
Frank Porteus
Dr. David H. White, PhD
John H. Stone III

Front Cover: Dr. Joe from Virginia looks at multiple Clapper rail birds jumping from the Spartina marsh grass, during a flood tide as the skiff is being poled. NC wilderness Spartina grass flats lay inside that state's coastal barrier islands and are only accessible at the highest of tides. **(Shawn Bennett photo)**

Back Cover: Joe Guide and his client- Mr. Ray of Charlotte, N.C., had a great day in de' Morning; one flood tide day in September's early rail bird season, off the Lower Cape Fear River's flooded salt marsh. It was Ray's very first traditional rail bird hunt.

DISCLAIMER

This book was written to provide information in regard to the history of rail bird hunting. Rail bird hunting in the United States occurs in both salt and fresh water marshes and estuaries, and a book such as this, was never intended to be a substitute for good judgment or common sense. Nevertheless, every one of my readers must venture into their home waters at their own risk! Therefore, this outdoor book should be used only as general rail bird hunting, a history of these species, and as a travel guide, but *not* as your *only source* of information on hunting, gunning, boating or travel.

Always wear a PFD when you are on the water, and always keep your shotgun cased when traveling. When you are ready to hunt, ensure your shotgun is on safe, or unloaded, except until you are actually ready to do some shooting. Common sense is sometime uncommon. Always be safe.

Many *guides*, towns and communities, as well as shotguns, boats, shotgun shells, and motors have been listed and discussed in this book. However, except where I have expressly mentioned it, *a listing in this book* is in *no way* to be considered *a recommendation* by either the author or the publisher.

Be safe whenever you are boating, and especially every time you are hunting. The purpose of this book is to educate. Safe and effective wildfowl hunting is the key to enjoyment and future success, just as much as scouting areas well prior to the hunting season, and understanding the tides and migratory patterns. These points are vastly important for success in gunning rail birds in your home waters and marshes. As a Saltwater Fly Fishing guide, I get to see the rail birds nesting, and their hatchlings, and clutches, and baby rail birds at various stages of their development. It is simply amazing to gaze upon these wilderness backcountry waters and marshes along the coastal extremes of our great nation.

The author and the publisher shall have *neither* liability, nor responsibility to any person, or business, with any loss or damage caused, or to have alleged to have been caused, directly or indirectly, through any information contained in this book.

DEDICATION

To my wife Marilyn, and my children: Nikki, Grier and little John, who were baptized first in the faith, and second from a duck and rail bird boat; and to every wildfowler that grew up along the flyways of North America, who after their first rail bird hunt have come to appreciate hunting the noble but elusive members of the *Rallidae* family: the Atlantic Flyway's King rail, the distinctive Marsh Hen (Clapper rail), the diminutive Virginia rail, and the numerous little Sora rail birds that pass through our lives and our local marshes throughout their migratory seasons each year.

I believe that in this century, greater number of wildfowlers will learn to hunt rail birds due to the publication of the Rail Bird Hunter's Bible. They will get outdoors, become more active in organizations that sustain our public marshes and rivers for future hunting, and experience a few flood tide days of gunning, each and every season of their lives, such joys in the great outdoors. I hope that you, the reader, will book a trip and take a seat in the *gunner's chair* of a *traditional rail bird hunt* somewhere along the *Atlantic Flyway,* where history remains intertwined with our lives, our families, and our friends and communities who first introduced us to rail bird hunting, and to this grand sporting adventure.

Joe Guide Outfitters™ vehicle sticker (2010 Nikki D graphic design)

CONTENTS

ACKNOWLEDGEMENTS ix

PREFACE xiii

UNDERSTANDING MIGRATORY PATTERNS xxv

INTRODUCTION xxxiii

CHAPTER ONE: THE HISTORY OF MARSH HEN [RAIL] HUNTING 1

CHAPTER TWO: THE ATLANTIC FLYWAY 11

CHAPTER THREE: RAIL BOATS, MOTORS & PUSH POLES 17

CHAPTER FOUR: SHOTGUNS, SHELLS, & ACCESORIES 25

CHAPTER FIVE: RETRIEVING DOGS 31

CHAPTER SIX: ENVIRONMENTAL ISSUES IMPACTING RAIL BIRDS, THEIR HABITAT, BREEDING, AND FEEDING AREAS, AND HUNTING 37

CHAPTER SEVEN: BOATS, MOTORS, & OTHER HUNTING GEAR 53

CHAPTER EIGHT: RAIL HUNTING THE NORTHEASTERN STATES 59

CHAPTER NINE: MIDDLE ATLANTIC STATES: MARYLAND, DELAWARE, VIRGINIA 79

CHAPTER TEN: SOUTHEASTERN REGION: NORTH CAROLINA, SOUTH CAROLINA, GEORGIA, AND FLORIDA 85

RECIPES AND COOKING 101

ABOUT THE AUTHOR 105

BIBLIOGRAPHY & SCHOLARLY SOURCES 111

October rail bird flood tide skiffs-tossing markers, wooden pushpoles

Low country coastal sunrise; photo by Scott Loudermilk

Railbird shooting; traditional method

ACKNOWLEDGEMENTS

I am certainly grateful to all those rail bird hunters, researchers and biologist from all across our great nation, and from Canada, who reached out to my questions and requests in papers, and magazines, and word of mouth for all interested in rail bird hunting, or those who have participated in researching this book on rail bird hunting in the USA, and took the time and effort to contact me. You know who you are, and how kind many of you have been to me.

I started this study between deployments to Afghanistan, continued after I returned from a Pakistan deployment, and finished it well after my retirement. All those who sent photos to me are listed in the photos section if I used their photos, and many are my own unless noted. I am grateful to all those colleagues in the U.S. Fish and Wildlife Service who have helped me in some unique way over the years by answering my questions and providing me with some data. To all those in the Bird Banding Division who were most kind to me throughout the years, and all those individuals who answered or returned my calls and emails, or pointed me to someone who might provide me a more in-depth perspective due to their unique field or sub-specialty; I am thankful to have met you, spoken with you, quoted you, or learned something new from your part of the nation.

All researchers or journalists such as I enjoy opening other doors of knowledge, which allowed me to meet some new people, who may then be called friend or colleague. For all these individuals, I am thankful and honored to have known you, and listened to your thoughts and perspectives over the years of putting this book together.

Thomas Eakins- RAIL BIRD Shooter- oil on canvas- 1888

Hunter tries to walk up some Clapper Rails during incoming tide

Ed from Savannah, GA, had a good opening day rail bird hunt

PREFACE

Rail bird hunting can be summed up with these three words: it is *addictive*. If you've never been on a traditional rail bird hunt, you will soon learn about the four huntable species of rail birds that are quite numerous, and how each species is distributed throughout all the Flyways across North America. I will talk more in depth about the history of each of these four Eastern species that have healthy populations along the Atlantic Flyway: the Clapper, Virginia, Sora, and the King, as well as the locations where they can be found in larger numbers at various migratory periods of the year, and how best to get out and hunt them effectively and safely.

I will also discuss these four rail birds' ecology and breeding studies, and especially the various efforts made to learn more (good and indifferent) about this unique, migratory and huntable species, such as the state of California's DNR, and the USDFW's lack of scientific rail bird banding studies.

The State of California has spent millions of tax dollars trying to bring the endangered California King Rail (CKR) back to life. However, my readers will soon realize this species was not affected by hunting pressure, but by a multitude of ecological disasters that were aligned with development of many different factors. Complex housing and golf course management practices, along with early wastewater drainage issues into the delta marshes, combined with the invasion of the Norwegian rat that grew at an alarming rate throughout the Sacramento Delta marshes—and the failure of CDNR or the USDFW to control the rat's growth rate in that region of the rail birds' marsh breeding areas, which was not realized at that time, were the root causes and important factors leading a decrease in marsh bird hatch rates in that flyway throughout the years.

All these environmental issues took a toll upon that particular California King Rail bird's breeding activity in the region's marshes, especially from the 1950s to the 1980s. The environmental impact upon breeding rail birds eventually destroyed vast breeding populations of rail bird species along this particular breeding region of the Great Bear State of California, and contributed to placing the CKR on the endangered list and stopping all rail bird hunting in the state. What a hard lesson in environmental protection of one unique species.

Yet in all that time, there were only two years of bird banding studies performed for all the rail bird species in the Pacific Flyway by the USDWF Bird Banding division, which makes you wonder: Why does the state of California spend millions to save the endangered CKR, yet not press for bird banding program for all that state's huntable rail species, or at least attempt to trap and band some CKR to try to determine its full migratory range? Rail birds are smarter than other marsh birds, due to their migratory instincts and the environment in which they live–the heavy marshes of fresh and salt water endemic to each of the huntable species. We must learn about that, as well as each species, if we are to fully understand its migratory ranges, and its primary and secondary food sources, and overall become more educated hunters and birders, and more appreciative of our outdoor and public marshes throughout all seasons of the year.

Of course the Pacific Flyway is an exceptional migratory waterfowl flyway, and quite healthy in most of those populations that breed in Canada's providences and migrate southward each fall. However, when it come to larger populations of huntable rail birds in North America, or the United States of America, one must always return to the greatest of regions: the Atlantic and Mississippi Flyways. Here you find vast food sources all along these flyways, and quite healthy breeding populations with millions of migrating rail birds each fall and spring—especially along the Atlantic coastal inshore marshes, both fresh and salt.

Husband and wife's first Marsh Hen hunt with JOE GUIDE OUTFITTERS-Wilmington, NC. (2005)

Another factor contributing to the rail birds' massive growth rate since the Great Depression years has been a reemergence of fresh water food plots, which produce more rice, soybeans, and corn, along with buckwheat and other items planted by wealthy landowners. Many 501(c)3 non-profits, which are really mega-business entities, politely impact breeding and staging waterfowl, funded by corporations and private individuals who love and appreciate hunting waterfowl and wildfowl across the USA and Canada. Mexico's DU projects are also present; however, Mexico has been an environmental disaster when it comes to wastewater treatment and environmental disasters. I have my doubts that anything south of El Norte will have a positive impact on rail bird growth.

The Rail Bird Hunter's Bible is the first hunting book on rail birds ever written in the United States. Articles had been written about the Sora rail and hunting in the rice meadows of the Northeastern United States' fresh water rivers and lakes since a publication in the Boston, MA, outdoors magazine in September 1852, which was republished later in December of 1853. However, noted ornithologist John James Audubon comments about the Mud Hen and all the species of the rail bird throughout his personal journals, observing and taking part in hunting trips for these rail bird species as early as 1809, although parts of those journals did not get unto the greater public view until 1843.

Brooke Meanley's wonderful biological studies of *The Marsh Hen* in 1985 broke new ground for scientific researchers. Nevertheless, he limited himself in this particular study primarily to the Middle Atlantic, South Atlantic and the brackish marshes of Cameron Parish. These were also my stomping and fly fishing grounds throughout many adventures in hunting and fishing, and observing wildlife and ecology. I visited Cameron Parish (and all the coastal parishes of Louisiana) one year after Hurricane Katrina hit that state. I was very troubled by the ecological impact of so many boats and so much oil washed up throughout the salt marsh, as well as those items distributed throughout that unique ecosystem. In most recent reflection, the more modern disasters that negatively impact coastal ecosystems along the Gulf of Mexico, due to the oil pipeline explosion of the deep water pumping unit, have their own place in the history of environmental disasters impacting the natural resources and the locals' financial livelihood during the years-long cleanup and beyond.

Throughout my studies and research, I've tried to delve deeper into the history of all these huntable species and look not only at every scientific study, but every Hunter Information Program (HIP) Survey, USFW Migratory Bird Banding Program, the Migratory Bird Stamp, and any article or research paper ever written on the four huntable rail bird species across our great nation. I talked with wildfowlers (hunters and birders) from all the flyways that pursue these species. In that light, I wanted this book to be a unique, historical, and educational hunting and travel book, unlike any other wildfowl hunting book ever written, as I desire to look deeper into the history and mysteries of these particular rail bird species. I've included the people that pursue them with great passion, as well as the areas, photos, regions, states, flyways and communities—birders, hunters, and watermen, historians and researchers— and the environmental aspects that surround these sporting birds and impact them negatively and positively

The Clapper Rail (Rallus longirostris) is certainly the most dominant, vocal, and populous of all these unique subspecies in the USA. It is also known throughout the coastal communities that grew up in the mud and oysters, marshes and brackish as well as salt marshes along the whole Atlantic Coast, as the Marsh Hen, who seems to talk loudly at various times of the morning and evening hours in the salt marsh.

I hope that during this new century, we will see a new growth of rail bird hunters, from sea to shining sea, directly due to hunters pursuing these exceptional and tasty sporting birds a couple of flood tides each year. I believe more donations will be directed into breeding and banding programs in future years, due to my travels across the USA and to this book. I looked deep into rail bird feeding habitats, and the ecology and evolution of these species throughout their survival even during destruction of nesting areas due to spring storms, the evasive rat and mink, and other predators that prey upon their eggs. I looked deeper than any other outdoor writer into the various environmental aspects around the nation, and the lessons learned from those experiences.

This is not your normal hunting book, such as you might find in humorous sections of Outdoor Life or Sports Afield magazines—which, in my opinion, are not as vibrant or in-depth, or in tune with what the educated and wealthy outdoorsman who is willing and able to give to certain communities needs to know, in order to fund important causes they feel strongly about. These unique sporting migratory birds can inspire just as much passion as any waterfowler may feel about ducks and geese. I do, of course, talk about traveling to various locations, but I will never give GPS coordinates. Educated outdoorsmen seek to learn, to scout out new areas and travel to interesting areas to visit off season, and to hunt and fish in those seasons of the year.

I will talk about how rail bird hunters should best get out to the marsh at various seasons of the year, and how one should "properly" hunt rail birds for better success. I speak about individuals I have met, and historical figures who were sportsmen—and keen ones—in their day and time, and of the passions and financial successes of organizations such as **Ducks Unlimited** and **DELTA**. Each of you needs to take paper and pen, and the time to write to these particular organizations, and encourage them to increase research studies on the huntable species of rail birds, and invest in rail bird banding to better understand rail bird migratory patterns. This is another important key to improve rail birds' actual numbers, their growth rate, and wildfowl management of a species that is poorly understood, except by those who hunt them with a passion for a few days or weeks each year.

If you pursue this unique and sporting marsh bird with passion during our next season, or later in your life's adventures, in your home state's fresh water marshes or a neighboring state's coastal salt marshes, you will see for yourself why so many people who love rail bird hunting try to keep it a secret from the waterfowling community across the nation. You will soon realize just how addictive rail bird hunting can be. I thank all whom I've met throughout the four years spent working on this book. I hope you, the reader, will discuss it with your family and best friends, and get out rail hunting this next season.

Although numbering well in the hundreds of millions in the Atlantic and Mississippi Flyways alone, rail birds are quite a unique species. They are a webless, migratory sporting bird, and there are laws and regulations governing where, when, and how one hunts these species in their respective flyways—which, due especially to environmental conditions, are very different from other flyways. I talk about these things in this book. My friends at the Nature Conservancy and the Audubon Society, and that one old fellow who works for Ducks Unlimited—where they keep hidden away, deep in a little back office at one of their multi-million dollar buildings, research and analysis studies of migratory bird species—all these fellows would tell you that *six of the nine rail bird species that breed in North America* are found throughout the United States; and *all of these species are abundant and continuing to breed and grow at a excellent growth rate.* The only exception is the California King rail, which is unique to that state and the Pacific Flyway, and which since the 1970s has been an endangered species due to environmental issues relating to its breeding habitat.

However, I will say that the Atlantic King rail bird has shown a tendency to cross breed with Atlantic Clapper rail females, which has resulted in tremendous numbers of hybrid King/Clapper rails. This may be due to their migratory flock movement throughout the ages.

The USDFW Bird Band division has not focused enough money on banding Clappers, Sora's, and Virginias, nor Kings. The big money grants for migratory banding research go to waterfowl migratory management, and not to the lowly wildfowl sporting rail birds, but I hope that in due time the rail bird will become better respected by the wildfowl hunting community that pours in research dollars to the powers that be in Research and Development Analysis programs across all flyways.

These four huntable species—King, Clapper, Virginia, and Sora—are all masters at hiding in the marsh. This is quite true throughout all the flyways of the USA, not just my Atlantic Flyway, which has been for centuries the one area of the United States with the most rail bird hunters and the most traditional rail bird hunting via poling the skiff during a flood tide. You are aware that rail birds are secretive. The adults hang tight to cover in the marsh, the heaviest of cover, and only exit when the flood tides push them out. However, I must tell you that rail birds *per specie*, are the *kung fu elite* of all the sporting birds when it comes to hiding from sportsmen in the marsh. Their territorial habitat is always in the thickest of marsh, and only a flood tide can make them move out of cover.

Four huntable species are abundant and showing sustained growth in large numbers of rail birds (marsh hens). These are reported in HIP reports by hunters along the Atlantic Seaboard coastal marshes, and well inside the barrier sea islands' great marshes, and those that pursue them with a passion can always be found each September through December pushing or poling their skiffs or light boats in the marshes during the highest of the flood tides in each state's rail bird seasons. Traditionally, as one goes southward, they will find some states that choose later season dates because the migration of rail birds into their regions occurs later in the months of October, November and December. However, one still cannot get to them except during the flood tide periods occurring during the full and new moon lunar periods that influence tidal flooding of the salt marshes, along with an occasional strong NE winds that push tides a bit higher than normal at times.

Primarily, Clappers are found in great numbers along the coastal inshore marshes, and Sora's are mostly in the fresh water rice meadows in great numbers. Of course, the Virginias and Kings often turn up as well, more so along the salt marsh immediately following heavy cold fronts for a day or two. However, these two species are found more often in brackish marshes that lay closer to great freshwater rivers flowing into the Atlantic Ocean along the coast. Furthermore, you will never find any of these birds in great numbers unless you focus on flood tide days and times, and hunt them with the traditional method of polling a light skiff or rail boat through thick marshes during these periods.

History has shown that not many outdoor journalists have pursued traditional rail bird hunting methods, as they are very laborious for the poler. However, if you make the effort, you will most certainly get caught up in the excitement of the rail bird hunt!

In the southern coastal states, local watermen tend to simply refer to all rail birds as marsh hens. To be poled or pushed through a marsh in a light skiff during a flood tide along the Atlantic Flyway coastal states is unlike any other waterfowl hunting you will experience in your lifetime!

Audubon wrote about a classic Clapper rail hunt in 1831 and later bird hunt experiences in his *Birds of America* (1842). He referred to rail bird hunting in the traditional fashion as *the sport of kings*.

Another excellent first-person account of the Atlantic and Mississippi Flyway can be found in Nathaniel H. Bishop's *Voyage of the Paper Canoe (1876)*. This story dealt with a young man's experiences traveling the Eastern Seaboard in a paper canoe, and the people and wildfowl seen during his journey along the Atlantic coastal inshore waters, its inlets, and its coastal rivers.

Being an adventurous young man, Bishop journeyed once again. However, this time he took a Barnegat Bay boat down the Ohio and Mississippi River to New Orleans, and east along the Gulf to northwest Florida, an epic 2,600-mile journey described in his travel adventure book *Four Months in a Sneak-Box* (1873).

You should take the time and effort to read Audubon, as well as the pioneer Philadelphia ornithologist Alexander Wilson, who tramped throughout the freshwater and salt marshes along the northeast and southeast states. His great work, *American Ornithology* (1808-1814), is most interesting reading. Wilson devoted a great amount of study and time in the field to the New Jersey rice field meadows and coastal salt marshes. As other rail bird researches have realized, Wilson thought there was a close link between the Clapper and King rail. Wilson's own illustrations of the Clapper tend to favor the King rail's brownish plumage, yet Audubon felt that Wilson "considered the Clapper to be akin to an adult *Rallus crepitans,* and I tend to wonder if interbreeding of the Clapper/King species was just as dominant, depending on spring migration of those two species." This certainly deserves more consideration at least in light of research and analysis.

A light boat in Audubon's day was a light ash bateau, whereas today it's a light wooden skiff, or aluminum boat. Hunting sports are still pushed or poled amid incoming high tides in the salt marsh or along the fresh water marshes, just like they were back in the 1800s. Isn't that interesting? It still takes a lot of hard work and effort to hunt these birds, and that's just a few examples of why there are so many millions of these migratory rail birds throughout the Atlantic Flyway to the present day.

Today you can find a public salt marsh area, or a fresh water marsh, where it's legal to hunt rail birds throughout their migration period each fall if you follow the migratory game bird rules and regulations of your home state. Marsh hen/rail bird hunting is a great sporting adventure for today's outdoorsman and hunter, or for fathers and sons who seek to get back into the wilderness and experience a bit of traditional wildfowling history throughout our personal journey in life's great adventures, and in the modern sport of wildfowling in North America.

Rail bird hunting is a distinguished sport for the modern day wildfowler who may come from the city, the suburbs, or the countryside. It is an equal opportunity sport, too. A fellow using a $40,000 technical skiff has no great advantage over the sportsman pushing a 450-pound Jon boat when you are deep in the flooded spartina grass during a flood tide period Individuals, hunting the elusive marsh hens. Yes, it is certainly a labor-intensive sport, and a good rail bird guide is worth his weight in gold, but this unique wildfowl hunting sport has not changed very much since the 1850s, when the first shooting sports magazine article described it to the sportsmen and sportswomen of that day and time.

You must have certain important equipment in order to pursue this sport with success. As I mentioned, it's a labor-intensive sport, as there is a lot of pushing and poling necessary prior to getting set up in position. For a good shot, one must first push their boat into position. It is against the law to shoot rails while in a motorboat under power by any motor (outboard, inboard, or electric motor). Traditionally it's always about using a push pole to propel your skiff or boat through the back country marsh in pursuit of rail birds. It's an awesome experience of a lifetime, which captures the hearts and minds of the educated wildfowler today just as it did hundreds of years ago. What is simply amazing is that the difficulty of poling a boat stops many hunters from pursuing rail birds during their season of the year. There are some who want to walk the marsh, which can be quite dangerous business if you get stuck in suck mud or fall into a deep hole, Rail bird walk-up hunting always produces few results for your labors, since rails have a habit of disappearing like Harry Houdini. The rail birds of all species are master hiders, and perhaps 90% of kayakers hear but never see the Clapper rail, which is the most dominant and prolific of all six rail bird species in North America today.

The traditional rail bird hunt—with the wind at your back, and with *la bella Luna* increasing the height of the flooding tidal waters upon hundreds of thousands, if not millions of acres of salt marsh wilderness along the Atlantic and Gulf Coasts - can be a wonderful day. It certainly appeared so to Audubon, as well to the mere observer, that a salt marsh estuary system flushed by the tides and the very breath of God; that we as mere mortals can experience such a wonderful outdoors hunt. Each and every year I hunt across the USA, I continue to be amazed by the incredible abundance of rail birds that migrate along the most historical of flyways, the Atlantic Flyway. Their migrations southward along the eastern seaboard barrier island salt marshes continue to this day in the same fashion they have since the colonial days, when a young George Washington and his cousins shot marsh birds and wildfowl off the Potomac, and even along the James River's majestic delta marsh.

I've looked out through those two unique fresh water marshes, which are not in the greatest of environmental shape today, and yet further down, glancing out upon Fortress Monroe from that northwestern marsh off the Chesapeake Bay at flood tide, and I've wondered what sights have gazed across those walls and upon these marshes throughout the years? What hope for better days was pondered by the gunner in the forward chair, and the marsh hen guide standing at the back of a light wooden skiff while using a five-pound, 18-inch homemade ash push pole…the one used long ago on those same marshes? As for myself, I certainly prefer my modern day 18' STIFFY Graphite Guide's Edition Push Pole (www.stiffypushpoles.com), which weighs in at just 2.7 pounds.

To have gunned the great wilderness marshes across all the flyways of North America and love it as I have, and to use and enjoy its natural resources in the light of such sportsman's understanding and care as most of my readers realize is to fight keenly and fairly, whatever threatens to spoil those natural resources; how joyous it is, to share this with those closest to you—each and every golden and joyful season is indeed a blessing. Sportsmen: take heart of such things, and know we are blessed with our surroundings. In most states, hunting is a privilege, not a right, and we must always use common sense and be more active in educating the public through our rail bird hunting experiences if we wish to ensure this exceptional gunning sport continues to take root across our nation.

In my opinion, I believe that the labor-intensive aspects of hard poling in difficult marsh, and dealing with the variants of location, travel and tidal levels in various public rail bird hunting areas of the Atlantic Flyway, will slowly gather more and more dedicated rail bird hunters in the future. Nevertheless, that will take time.

Rail bird hunting is nothing like duck hunting. It is not that easy, and you will soon realize that rail bird hunting in the traditional manner takes much more effort. You must plan your hunts according to time and distance to the area, remaining aware of the migration patterns and the weather fronts that dominate these marsh birds' migration clocks. Many Americans are not able to hunt that many flood tide days due to work and family and financial aspects, and depending on where they live, people must travel some distance and make time to hunt rail birds during migratory periods, throughout various states where rail bird hunting is more prevalent.

It takes a special light boat, and a desire to scout, and travel, and put in time on the water during flood tides, and see for yourself the lay of the marsh at various times and seasons of the year. Of course, not every wildfowl hunter is willing or financially able to do this, except for perhaps a few days each season. It really takes a dedicated person and a desire to focus on the time and effort each sportsman has available, and the resources each sportsman has at hand. It also matters where they happen to live, as well as the financial resources that are available to them during the various seasons of the year.

Like life's great journey, rail bird hunters savor the experiences gained from simple joys, such as being pushed through rising tides that ebb and flow amid the migration of life that is seen all around us in a marsh. Like specks of sand pouring through an hourglass, so are the days of our lives upon this ol' world, and some experiences surely add up in terms of statue. In any real wildfowler's code of ethics and honor are one's experiences and lessons that are learned in pursuit of the noble rail bird, and yet ourselves, while pushing through a difficult flood tide of world events and distant memories of days afield. Rail bird hunting can be a surreal experience that most cannot comprehend until it is actually experienced firsthand in the wild. What lessons will you learn? I hope a great deal, as this book should be the *magnum opus* for all future books on rail bird hunting in North America.

When I was an undergraduate at the former USC Coastal, now Coastal Carolina University, my old Professor of Ancient Languages was The Rev. Doctor Robert W. Robinson, AB, MDIV, MAT, PhD who was at the time the assistant Dean of the Department of Philosophy and Religion at USC Coastal (now Coastal Carolina University, Conway, S.C.), and the only professor at that university who'd graduated from one of the colleges (Manchester) of Oxford, England. He would often quote Latin phrases to his students, reminding each of us of the brevity of life, and our place in our great journey through life's adventures, and the importance of educating both ourselves, and others. Dr. Bob began each lecture by stating these words, which are also engraved on my University ring: "*Emollit Mores Nec Sinit Esse Feros*". The English translation for this phrase is: *Learning humanizes character and does not permit it to be cruel.*

Those of my readers who may have earned your own red badge of courage, those who are called wounded warriors, and like me have seen death and chaos throughout times of peace, and during times of war, may realize, as I have—firsthand, over time—just how fragile all of life is. Yet in perspective, you also realize just how joyous life and friendships can be: that reunion of old' friends on a planned hunting trip, together once again in the great outdoors, and when good hunters and Labradors or retrieving dogs come together for a few days, each on some special outdoor adventure afield, and every season is upon hearts and minds like a sonnet.

When we hear that Clapper rail bird's laughing—*kak, kak, kak*—or a nervous Sora rail bird's *peep...peep...peep*, we rail bird hunters take joy in simple pleasures like a good hunt, good eating, good retrievers, a classic SxS or O/U, and the opportunity to get together again each year to go rail bird hunting. It is indeed a grand experience, out in the marsh during a cold front pushing through, or on a bright clear day during a flooding high tide in the marsh. You and your buddy, or you and your son, or your daughter, or your children's children, should experience one or two days like this each and every year.

Sora Rail

A gunner and his dog look for Rail birds as the tide floods into a Spartina Grass Flat

UNDERSTANDING MIGRATORY PATTERNS

Rallidae are most succinctly wildfowl, and are webless migratory rail birds of the family Rallidae. Being webless marsh birds, they hide very deeply and very effectively within the marshy jungles of low county cattails and coastal saltwater marsh grasses they call home. Depending on their migration location and weather conditions, rail birds enjoy both fresh and saltwater marshes. However, different species tend to prefer their traditional migration stopovers, and use these periods of rest for feasting heavily upon the primary and secondary food sources that are important to their migration needs. Sora and King Rail are always found in greater numbers in wild and cultured rice fields, and flooded fresh water marshes throughout their migration periods.

All four species of huntable rail birds are best hunted in fresh and saltwater marshes throughout the low country of the Atlantic, Mississippi, and Central Flyways—provided you seek them out with careful scouting during their migration periods. You must first learn to understand their migratory patterns, and then only through your efforts of slugging through marsh in a shallow draft jonboat, or a very light wooden rail boat with push pole after cold fronts, and during full moon periods will you find concentrations of rail birds for periods of time.

You must seek them out during flood tides, when they cannot keep hiding deep in the marsh grass. Depending on landowner permission, you might be lucky enough to get into a private rice field on a plantation by the coast, or a great farm with rice field impoundments. Or perhaps you may be not too far from a fresh water reservoir, lake, or river where wild rice meadows are located, and there you will find scads of rail birds in the early migration period—Sora if it's wild rice, perhaps a few Virginia rail birds, or if you are very lucky, some King rail birds.

Clappers and a handful of Sora rail birds can be found along the coastal salt marshes. These areas are populated mainly by Clappers, as they are healthy, breed well, and populate all along the Atlantic flyway coastal inshore waters in salt marshes that lie behind the barrier islands.

If you seek them out, and do enough scouting during key periods in September and October when the highest of tides are active, you will most assuredly find Clapper rail birds. You must watch the tides, and keep abreast of the cold fronts, too. When a cold front pushes through Canada along the north and northeast in October or November, you will soon find that new rail birds have pushed down into your area within two or three days.

Now, if there happens to be a terrible, nasty hurricane, that certainly changes things. You will soon find many species of rail birds pushed down the coast, trying to south and stay well outside the storm front. Any rail birds you find one day may very well not be there the following day, especially during a full moon period. However, if it's the week of a new moon, you will have some good high tides in October, but perhaps not in November. Or perhaps you may find that the new tide is better (higher) than the full moon tide that month, or that the highest tide occurs after shooting time (sunset) ends—and well, that really doesn't allow you to push that particular hunt due to flooding too late in the day.

However, if you find yourself somewhere along the Atlantic Flyway's coastal salt marsh, where public waters and marshes abound for miles on end, and you are smart enough to plan on scouting during a flood tide which will allow you to get out into those marshes and see exactly what rail birds are out there, and cover enough territory to ensure you have found enough birds, then you will be ready to have a great hunt when high tide happens the next day. You've just got to make the time and do the work to find where the rail birds are, and then get out there and push 'em up that next flood tide while the birds are there. You need to become familiar with tide charts and the marsh areas that are most productive in your area for rail birds.

One thing you must realize is that the place where you found those rail birds one week last year may not be the same place where you're going to find lots of rail birds the following year, even during the same full moon or new moon period. If you have wild rice, and there is not a lot of wild rice a hundred miles or so, then you'll probably always have enough Sora rail birds until their migration leaves your regional area due to bad weather, or until the majority of the food is depleted.

I think it's good that people have to work at finding the rail birds, and that you cannot fully know how long they are going to be in a certain area. In the salt marsh, you don't know if the rail birds are going to stay for one day, or three days. However, do you know the parameters of the tidal variance in that particular salt marsh? What does it take to properly flood it? How long does the tidal high last when the wind is pushing from various directions? You must understand that some winds will impede the flood tide somewhat, and other winds will increase the tidal height due to lunar implications. Then there are storms, cold fronts, and other factors to consider.

It pays to understand your hunting area, your marshes. My buddy JP Hand told me that some people get caught up chasing rail birds in the high wild rice, and can easily ignore the falling tide. This puts them at risk of being stuck and unable to pull their boats out to the nearest creek, or cut to deeper and safer water. Do your homework early, and study your hunting areas if they are tidal. Are there stumps? Be careful.

It is always important to play it safe, ensure you know all the exits when you are in charge of your boat in a hunting area, and understand what the limitations are in hunting some areas over other areas, whenever you go rail bird hunting. It's no fun getting stuck in the marsh, any marsh. Be alert, and do your homework when you do your scouting. You will have a limited tidal window of opportunity in which you can hunt certain areas when birds are present, and all these factors are important. Then you must factor in the wind direction, or rain, or a cold front.

In September, you might have a thunderhead, or a hurricane or terrible cold front may be heading your way, which will close out your hunting when it causes most of the rail birds to get the hell out of Dodge, and fly south for nicer territory and food sources. Like humans, they are not going to hang around when a hurricane or a bad storm front is pushing down their way.

Understanding migratory patterns is a vastly important aspect in the great puzzle of learning the intricacies of rail bird hunting and any new marsh complex. Migratory birds will most certainly move—that's just something all migratory fowl do for several reasons, whether it's food, a safe haven, a lack of pressure, or too much pressure. All those factors come into play, and must be considered to better understand migratory game birds such as rail birds. There can be a great many reasons why you'll find birds in some locations, and other locations may not have as many. Rail birds do not necessary return to their old breeding grounds to feed during their migration periods in the fall. That is not always the case. However, it could be that they will return to feed in an area that's one, two, or a few more miles away when they pass through those same areas they know very well throughout the southern coastal inshore waters, if they wintered over during their migration periods.

One thing is certain: ail birds will return to wherever the food has been, but will not tarry if the food sources have been depleted. They will quickly move somewhere else. Find the food sources, and you will find the rail birds. Look for their major food sources: invertebrates, seeds, and wild rice. Look for heavy cover, brackish water for Virginia rail, fresh water for Kings and Soras, and salt marshes for Clappers. I like to keep areas updated with maps and coordinates. They always change. Sometimes not so much, sometimes drastically—yet certain factors are more important if you know what you're looking for when you are scouting a hunting area. Sometimes I have one hour to search a few thousand acres of salt marsh.

Food is one key. However, it could be prediction in some areas. You must surely do your share of scouting if you desire a high-yield rail bird hunt. There is no better way to ensure you have a great hunt than to put in the hours of scouting out the marshes and find out exactly where new birds are located. Sometimes I will find more Sora in certain locations, and others I may find few to no Soras around during their migratory periods.

You must either seek them out by scouting the areas well before the seasons of the year, or find a reputable rail bird guide., Those fellows are really few in number, and can be quite hard to get a booking with. The very best ones are known through word of mouth, and they all have special rail boat rigs for gunning. You'll want the best experience you can get, so try to set up a guide trip during only the highest of high tide days, with a good guide that has all the gear, knows his particular area or marsh and tides, and keeps up with the migration. Or you can get all your own gear, put in the hours and travel, and put forth the efforts of trial and scouting yourself.

Rail bird shooting is traditionally done with a knowledge guide who uses a light, shallow-draft skiff or Jon boat, and launches well before the highest of the flood tides in a saltwater marsh complex where rail birds are most numerous along the coastal inshore waters of the Atlantic Flyway. Here, the Clapper rail rules the marsh, and the little Sora (which often migrates together with the King) are found in even greater numbers throughout the thousands of miles of exquisite salt marshes and Spartina grass flats, where only when the Prince of Tides with all his mighty lunar efforts comes to push them out of the depths of their wilderness abode during just a few sweet days each month, when the highest of the high new and full moon flood tides can be found.

As I've mentioned, these are the primary rail bird shooting periods along any coastal waters. Fall month flood tide periods are influenced by the New Moon lunar periods, but they are also impacted by some excessive northeastern and northern cold fronts that drive winds into shallow, low country salt marshes, pushing water out of shallow bays and into the marshes. When this happens, it tends to increase the periods of tidal highs especially during October and November, into something of a super high tide of around 2 to 4 inches greater than the tide which is actually projected.

I've found excellent hunting when a massive front pushes through the coastal marshes, even on a simple 5.2 H/T—which, due to those conditions, may more resemble a 5.8 inch flood tide. You've just got to understand how to read a Doppler radar and in understanding wind and tidal variations, instead of always relying on some person on your local the weather channel. Do you want to trust a TV meteorologist who is 100, or 25 miles away from your weather? I utilize many different variables and see for myself what the flood tide and weather are like. The forecast may call for 28 mph gale force winds off shore, but in reality it might end up with inshore winds in the low twenties. The wind must be your friend in the salt marsh.

My friends, it is days such as those that make a grand rail gunning day in the marsh—epic in quality, and memorable throughout time whenever Lady Luck, and general averages come together to visit your neighborhood salt marsh flats during a flood tide, when the rail birds are hunkered down. Those are mighty special days to be out rail bird hunting. Such super high tides allow rail bird hunters two hours or more of a good tidal period, in order to use push pole and skiff to seek out and hunt rail birds through the best of our coastal wilderness salt marshes.

Weather being what it can be, with warmer falls becoming more and more common, I could be out on the Maurice River in Southeastern New Jersey in 72-degree weather in September, or in October , and experience weather much like Charleston, South Carolina, in early December before their 2d split of the SCDNR rail bird season closes. Super high tide days are quite limited, as you can imagine, happening only three or four days each full or new moon period. Yet all the factors can come together in place, and perhaps there will even be a Nor'easter pushing through. In these situations, a local guide who works the great marshes, and keeps up with the movement of the rail bird migrations is worth their weight in gold. The very best rail bird guides are traditionally booked solid for most, if not all, of the super high tide days throughout the rail bird gunning season along the Atlantic Flyway, where the more traditional rail bird hunting exists today as it did when it was first reported to the public readers of outdoor magazines and sporting journals in the 1850s.

Friends, if each of you rail hunters today will make an supreme effort to take a young person out rail bird hunting this season, you will most assuredly contribute to these young fellows' education as sportsmen and women, and share in their sporting development, in the enjoyment of the great outdoors, and wildfowling in general. The future of rail bird hunting will become richer through your efforts, and you will secure for all our children's children the pursuit of this great natural resource that we hunters enjoy in the remaining public wilderness areas that still exist in our home states, and coastal low country, and throughout all the impoundments, marshes and flyways of the United States.
I encourage each of you to support Ducks Unlimited and Delta Waterfowls unique marshland Restoration Programs throughout the USA and Canada. These two organizations actively support and develop innovative marsh and delta wetlands improvement and reclamation projects which positively impact each migratory species of Rallidae throughout their breeding and migration periods.

Remember that our sport is a privilege, not a right, and we are supposed to be trustees of this great tradition of gunning wildfowl throughout North America today.

In conclusion, I hope each of you will remember the words of the mighty Nimrod, and conservationists, and rail bird hunters throughout our nation's history: John J. Audubon, President Grover Cleveland, President William Henry Harrison, Theodore Roosevelt, George Bird Evans, T. Nash Buckingham, Phil Robertson, and Joe Guide; these words that should be within our hearts and minds: "…the youth of today and tomorrow, are the future of wildfowling in North America!"

All four species of rail bird–Nikki Dinkins Illustraton–2013

INTRODUCTION

Down south, we still call all of 'em *marsh hens* throughout Atlantic Coast, and along the rice fields and marshy fresh water impoundments fringing the Mississippi Flyway. Nevertheless, rail bird hunting seems to be the perennial "red-headed step child" of the wildfowl community. These sporting birds should get more respect from the wildfowl community, and organizations such as Ducks Unlimited, Delta Waterfowl. I strongly believe that more federal funding should be appropriated by the US Department of Fish and Wildlife's Bird Banding Division for more banding studies for these four huntable species of rail birds.

I hope this book will encourage my readers to lobby for these four migratory species through more rail bird band studies. Here are just a couple of interesting facts and figures in researching bird banding data IRT clapper and sora rail birds. According to R.E. Stewart's 1954 banding study, he found a recovery rate of 4.5% for Clapper rails which were banded at Chincoteague, Virginia. Of those forty-six Clapper rail birds that were captured and banded, Stewart found that forty-five birds were killed by hunters—and one was run over by a car!

Forty-two clapper rail birds were taken during the first hunting season, all within four months following these particular birds' banding log entries. Of special note was that one immature Clapper rail bird banded on July 3, 1933, in an earlier banding study was shot and recovered by rail bird hunters during that bird's fourth hunting season on October 29, 1936. Surely the fastest migration study had to come from a 1971 Sora rail bird, captured and banded in Cape May, N.J., and shot by a rail bird hunter outside Charleston, South Carolina—the very next day! (*Major Ben Moise, SC, DNR; interview with the author*)

Yet for those across our great nation—dedicated wildfowlers who appreciate the great effort, logistics, travel, and determination that go into traditional rail bird hunting, who have known for centuries just how great this wildfowl hunting is, and who really do not wish to see more hunters in the public marshes—it is essential that its popularity continues. All along the Atlantic Flyway, especially in coastal New Jersey and throughout the Southern Atlantic tidal marshes, the full and new moon high tides and favorable winds bring dedicated generations of wildfowlers again and again for traditional flood tide rail bird hunts. This is a dedicated group of sportsmen who enjoy old and renewed friendships and unique guides, shotguns, and handmade rail boats, and pray for fair winds and super high tides which can extend their hunting opportunities along the tidal marshes.

As I've mentioned, rail bird hunting shall always remain a true gentlemen's sport. It was first described by J.J. Audubon in his travel and hunting journal notes, especially during his southern visits to friends in Charlestown, S.C., during September 1809, and during his extensive travels down the Mississippi and Missouri rivers during the fall of 1811. Audubon discussed many of his experiences and adventures, such as seeing the Great Haley's Comet and experiencing the great "New Madrid Earthquake," while he was traveling on one of the first great steamboat trips headed south to New Orleans. His entries were written while tied up off the river flow that very night, and discussed what he learned through his own experiences, as well as through talking with people and hunters and trappers all along his stops going down Ol' Miss. You would find his journal entries quite amazing, as I have.

AN EARLY OUTDOORS ARTICLE ON RAIL BIRD SHOOTING

Throughout the Northeastern states, there appeared an early article from the Boston newspaper *Gleason's Pictoral*, dated Saturday December 3, 1853, about rail bird hunting on the Maurice River. The article described a "traditional Sora rail bird hunt" with guides who pushed their "Sports" through tide-flooded meadows along the river, where wild rice grew in massive quantities and the stands were higher than your head during the month of September. Very soon, more and more wealthy sportsmen started taking the train to distant locations to hunt throughout the Northeastern states, from Merrymeeting Bay's wild stands of rice in Maine, to the Great Rice Meadows below the city of Essex, Connecticut, along that river, and especially along the Maurice River in New Jersey, as well as the coastal inshore waters of the middle Atlantic and the southeastern regions of the Eastern Seaboard. This was especially so after 1868, when more and more northern sportsmen and their close friends founded grand hunting club houses along the Atlantic Flyway from Maine to Florida. The popularity of the train excursions encouraged more sport hunting, and the increase in personal wealth and more favorable distribution of wealth due to the Industrial revolution assisted this growth.

Rail birds are migratory in nature, and they begin moving from Canada's marshes ever southward, staying just long enough to eat and store up fat and strength. Further migration of their species occurs normally in the month of August, as both small and large flocks of rail birds of various species move *en masse* during the nights of the full moon, and sometimes later if not threatened or when approaching cold front even signals in the northern states during September and October. With changes in the ancient weather patterns of the jet stream, hunters have been seeing more wintering over in the Clapper, the hybrid varieties of the King rail, and the Virginia rail along the Southern Atlantic coastal inshore marshes.

Rail bird hunting's early popularity developed eventually into the "sport of kings" as wealthy and famous individuals took up the sport and recreated it in the hotels and Bed and Breakfasts that sprung up near these hunting areas. Rail bird hunters today come from all backgrounds one could imagine, but in the late 1800s prior to and after the Civil War, enthusiasts included captains of industry, bluestocking sporting gentlemen, and individuals from Wall Street and banking backgrounds, sporting personalities, artists, and writers from all the best families of New Haven, Hyde Park, Philadelphia, Trenton, Portland, Bangor, Washington DC, Richmond, and Baltimore.

You would might find Wall Street types, doctors, and lawyers alike, and these fellows utilized their wealth derived from the financial success of the Gold Standard, oil and railroads, Wall Street trading, and most of the growth and development that came first and primarily from the Industrial Revolution. Much later, including the years of the great Civil War, these self-made men, whose families were worth millions in pre-tax dollars supplied the Civil War machines, and other businesses, and trusts and overseas trading. These were families who loved the great outdoors and the fellowship of sporting lives, and whole generations spent lifetimes building big businesses—dynasties, really—and continued their sporting endeavors anew, just as their fathers and grandfathers had enjoyed hunting trips and visiting for days, weeks, or months at a time on grand wildfowling adventures.

These were lessons passed down from father to son. Some of the great hunting lodges that still survive were built near where the members hunted, and were designed and built in the grand style of the day, and put a great number of locals to work. Some of these grand clubs in southern states like Virginia, North Carolina, and South Carolina, such as North Carolina's magnificent Whale Head Hunt Club located off the Outer Banks, did not have any southern members on their membership rolls until well into the 1950s!

Each September and October, fathers and sons and close friends especially would take some grand adventures afield, gunning for rail birds in Maine, Connecticut, New Jersey, and the Carolinas, being pushed by the Prince of Tides and local watermen who knew their rivers and marshes and rice meadows like the backs of their hands. These sportsmen were also political forces of nature who loved to hunt waterfowl and wildfowl in the company of their closest friends, in the tradition that they had grown up and been accustomed to, with the famously well-to-do. Some of their fathers had built "great hunting estates" in far-off regions along the coast from north to south.

For a more detailed history of these clubs along the Atlantic Seaboard, look at the books listed on Amazon that have been researched and written about the Great Wildfowl Hunting Clubs throughout the years.

These sporting folk enjoyed the fellowship of their best friends, and developed the growth of grand hunt clubs, properties, and homesteads in the coastal areas where they enjoyed hunting waterfowl and wildfowl. Some individuals did not forget their local communities where the hunting clubs were located and contributed massive sums of money toward community betterment, along with the development of schools and better education facilities for families who lived in the surrounding countryside. This was a time of great philanthropic gifts to communities, education, the arts, and medical facilities too. These same sportsmen contributed to the growth and movement of larger businesses, from the Northeast to the South Atlantic states, because of these sporting relationships and hunting visits, and the kindness shown to them by Southerners and their families through loyalty and common family values.

Wealthy gentlemen sought out hunting experiences and locations where they might enjoy traditional hunting pursuits with their fellow sportsmen in their unique community of friends all along the coastal states. Other like-minded individuals heard the stories of the most famous of rail bird hunting areas throughout this regional area, where one could take an afternoon train and enjoy a weekend hunt with their neighbors and friends. Coastal communities, hotels, and local watermen profited from these hunt clubs and the natural resources in their areas, and watermen started guiding for the hotels and sporting clubs, some of which paid guides more in one weekend than they could possibly earn in a month of traditional hunting.

Well before waterfowl migration come the marsh birds, the rail birds, and to get to them takes some effort and unique boats and poling, and keeping up with the vast migration. It therefore shows the reader that this manner of wildfowl hunting is a labor-intensive sport, which calls for the hardiest of guides and light skiffs. The really good guides cost a pretty penny. Even back in 1853, a good rail bird guide pushing a rail skiff on the Connecticut River rice fields out from Old Sayle could command a twenty-dollar gold piece for his boat and labors for a one-sportsman, four-hour rail bird hunt (approximately $350 today), whereas a common laborer in New York City's "bluestocking district" earned a whopping thirty-five cents an hour during that same time period, due to the Industrial Revolution's increases in labor costs.

Marsh birds stage for the great southern migration as far north as Canada's Maritime providences and the great James Bay marsh region, and begin their early migration southward during the full moon of August, sometimes lingering into September full moon week. These rail bird species tend to migrate primarily during the nights of a full moon, and move along that most ancient of flyways: the Atlantic Flyway. Over the last four years while researching *The Rail Bird Hunters Bible*, I have enjoyed interviewing numerous watermen, rail bird hunters, birders, guides, and fishermen—most in their fifties and sixties, many in their eighties, and a few even in their nineties. Each were quite unique in their backgrounds, and some of their families have resided in the same area since pre- and post-Colonial time. They described how while they were out in the rivers and bays working their nets, or fishing during the nights of the August full moon week, they would suddenly hear a rush of wings overhead, or nearby, and see the shadows of hundreds, thousands, and sometimes what appeared to be hundreds of thousands of rail birds migrating into the Maurice River, or the Delaware bay rice fields, or other locations in those regions. I heard similar statements from fishermen on Minnesota lakes that also have wild rice. Later, in passing the large rice meadows along these rivers on their way to the boat landings, they heard a cacophony of Sora rail birds—singing and talking to one another, calling hither and yon—where there had been no birds seen or heard earlier that day. (Walter Dinkins Research Journal Book #7: *New Jersey Maurice River: Railbird History: Interviews of guides, hunters + watermen*).

Even as far back as the early Colonial periods, there appeared accounts of migrations in late August throughout the southeastern and Mississippi flyways after the introduction of rice crops into irrigated fields. The first major migratory birds that came calling was the little and numerous Sora rail, in large and sometimes massive flocks, to gorge themselves on the sweet wild rice fields. These were followed by the other rail bird species as they moved ever southward to their wintering grounds along the Carolinas, coastal Georgia, and Florida's inshore marshes.

Moving through Maine with the cusp of the full moon in the month of August, and later that month into East Coast states pushing southward, sporting men and women pursued the four huntable Atlantic Flyway species: the Sora, Clapper, Virginia, and King rail birds that migrate from Canada's fresh water and coastal marshes down Maine's famous Merrymeeting Bay rice meadows, along the fresh water rivers of the Atlantic Seaboard inshore of the barrier islands, and to their traditional stopovers, since the beginning of time itself as those species developed. It was always a gentleman's gunning sport in coastal Virginia, North and South Carolina, where the major species was the larger Clapper rail bird.

Come September, waterfowlers feel a churning desire to unlimber that old side-by-side shotgun from the recesses of their gun safe and get out once again in a light skiff to pole deep into the far recesses of the wilderness of the salt marsh. There you can clear the cobwebs of your mind and learn to enjoy the sport of kings—hunting rail birds in our day and age with the greatest of ease, if you focus on only gunning the highest of tides. You and a buddy will certainly get some serious exercise while poling a skiff, or paddling a kayak, and shooting some rails during the September to November high tides. You will find that the local marsh may have a nice crop of rail birds out there just waiting to test you and your good ol' retriever as you hunt for rails in the backcountry salt marsh wilderness that still exists as public waters.

The marsh bird is a member of the Rallidae family. Clapper and Virginia rails are the most numerous of all rail birds found in the salt marsh, as the Clapper with their laughing voices cry out *Kak, kak, kak*. Bag limits are a generous 15 bird limit.

If you are looking in fresh water deltas, you'll mostly find the small, yellow-billed Sora rail (25 bird limit) which will "peep," and there is the larger King rail, which you will only find in fresh water, and only if you are extremely lucky. I normally will find a number of them mostly off the old Cooper River's wild rice fields during the highest of flood tides, in the months of November and December. Up north, you will find that there are literally thousands and thousands of Sora rail birds in the fresh water flood tides of the wild rice meadows off the Connecticut River, and New Jersey's Walking and Maurice Rivers in the Northeast.

Rail birds are marsh birds, and it takes dedication and hard work to get at them, as they all live, and breed, and hide deep in the marsh grass. Of all the species, it is the Clapper rail that is heard more often, by people when paddling through a marsh in the mornings or late evenings. However, they are not often seen, as they are masters of cover and can hide quicker than any wildfowl known to man.

When pressed, rail will run first, and I can assure you that any juvenile or adult rail can do a "thirty-yard dash" through the thickest of Spartina and gnarly marsh grasses in less than 90 seconds. Afterward, they'll take to water and swim to the next clump of thick marsh grass. Adult birds will take wing, only when they are well out of cover. It may surprise you that it took Audubon more than just a few shots with his shotgun in order to obtain his first rail, but it took him longer just to find it in the marsh grass. His painting of the Clapper and Sora (Carolina) rail are quite beautiful, and came from his first rail hunt down in Charleston, South Carolina, in the early fall of 1831.

When we attempt to relive the experiences of our own youth and recapture moments, lost in time, or when we visit places that were important to us and our families throughout our travels in the fall or summertime, many of us will return to the great Atlantic seaboard coast, with their miles of barrier islands and great marshes, powerful tides and winds. That coastline is truly massive, running from Maine down to Florida, and I hope you get to live to see many of these areas as I have seen them throughout the years, chasing rail birds throughout the marshes and the flyways across our nation in the years it took me to put this book together. This is the first book ever written on rail bird hunting in America.

The best and finest way to hunt rail birds is the traditional, or old school way. You'll need a shallow draft boat, a long push pole, a positive attitude, and a side- by-side shotgun. Pick your favorite gauge: .410, 20, or 28 ga shotgun. When observed in their salt marsh wilderness jungle land amid floating dead grass mats in a flood tide, they will appear to the birder—or the hunter wearing "black and white striped underpants," as my first paddler and rail hunting guide emeritus, Mr. Thomas T. Tomilin, said. Mr. Thomas grew up not far from Yellow House Creek on the Cooper River's old wild rice fields. He took me after rail birds not far from John's Island, and later on Hamlin Sound's salt marshes in the South Carolina low country.

He described "marsh chickens" to me on a chilly October flood tide day in October 1968, as a ten-year-old novice rail hunter who was shooting my papa's most expensive shotgun he ever bought. It was a beautiful 20 ga O/U Ithaca Model 500, and if I remember correctly, we were hunting with W.W. Bill Volletton, M.D., who was at that time the assistant dean of Ophthalmology at the Medical School of South Carolina down in Charleston.

An old motor boat was used to pull two guides and two wooden skiffs, with a cane back chair tied down at the front of each skiff, and we stopped upwind of the edge of a very large Spartina grass flat . Mr. Thomas would start poling me into the flooding salt marsh as I drank a cold RC Cola and munched on a Moon Pie. We were into rails very quickly, as it was an aggressive incoming tide. "Mighty powerful Northeastern pushing down from de' North," said Mr. Thomas. He pointed with his 18' push pole, crying out, "Dar de' is…see 'em' dar, running fast amid the grass mat." I missed my first two birds that jumped, as the winds were a brisk 18–20 knots that morning.

Rail birds tend to fly low and jump out of the marsh, much like a pheasant would in a cornfield- mostly with the wind, and the Clapper's would fly a good ways - across the salt marsh, with the wind in their little buttocks, only to clumsily appear to crash back to earth and take off like an Olympic sprinter, running like the devil in the deepest and thickest Spartina grass that God ever made. Clappers appear dusky brown, around 15 inches in height, with long legs built for speedy running, a curved little beak, often with grey and brown chest markings, and a turned-up tail that twitched a bit before they flushed. At first glance, their bottoms, looked like they were wearing striped underpants!

I hunted rails with the 1963 (16 yd New York State) 20 ga Trap Shooting Champion, Dr. Sidney B. Doolittle, M.D., who was one of the finest OB-GYNs that ever came out of Syracuse, New York. I was comforted somewhat when it took him 19 shots to get his limit of 15 Clappers one morning. Dr. Doolittle was quite a grand shot gunner, and that particular morning he was using a grand-looking Browning 20 ga O/U that had a beautiful Montecarlo stock. That gun was fitted with the first Briley screw in-choke tubes I'd ever seen, we hunted in later years with his youngest sons, Billy who was a mighty fine shotgunner too. I was saddened when he died at a young age due to an illness.

You've got to realize that rail birds will also use the wind to their advantage 90% of the time, whenever they jump, because they are certainly no dummies in their own marsh. It is a rare day, I tell you, when one of my clients can kill a limit of 15 rails with less than 19 shells! It has been done, of course, but it's not normal. Place yourself out on a trap field, when the wind is whipping up a storm, at the 16-yard mark back from the trap house. You'll see for yourself just how easy it can be to miss rail birds with a .410, 20ga, or 28ga. I don't care if you're gunning with one of those fancy automatics, or an SxS, or an O/U shotgun. It takes more than just having lady luck and general average on your hunt, everyone needs to take some practice on either the skeet or the trap field prior to the rail bird hunting season. Annie Oakley used to hunt quail in North Carolina in the fall each year in North Carolina's Pinehurst Community for more than twenty seasons. My grandfather and my Uncle Dink used to go occasionally to see her shoot in exhibitions prior to WWI. She would often tell the crowd that 90% of all misses on the skeet range or dove field or in wing shooting in general, were due to a gunner's failure to follow through on their right to lefts, and left to right- swing shots. Annie would stress the importance of both eyes open, and continued swing-through in wing shooting. I hope my readers can learn appreciate that lesson, and take it to heart next time they are out shooting rail birds, and their percentage would certainly increase, as would their confidence and shooting ability too!

Do you think of yourself as an exceptional shot? One who might possibly outshoot Annie Oakley, Herb Parsons, or Mark Arie on a good day? Perhaps you should think again! Here are some stats that you ought to take to heart, the average dove hunter with a twelve dove limit will average seven shots per bird killed. The average duck hunter will spend four hours to half a day for a six duck limit, and will average six shots per wildfowl killed. Diver hunters average 12 shots per diver killed on a bag limit of six ducks. Whereas rail bird hunters might average one bird per three or four shots, depending on winds, and rail bird hunters bag limit is 15 birds along the coastal Saltmarsh, and twenty-five sora rail in the fresh water rice field gunning. Of course, in rail bird hunting, as I have mentioned, is a more labor intensive sport than any other bird or waterfowl hunting, and that is due to the nature of the difficulty of the marsh and in getting out to where the rail birds are located, and it's altogether quite an adventure in hunting. You just cannot do it consistently by trying to walking em' up, in the marsh, because marshes are not conducive to that type of hunting. It's just too easy for the bird to hide, deep in the marsh, therefore, one must prepare to do it properly and using the "traditional method" for proper rail bird hunting- poling a light skiff or boat into the marsh where rail birds are located, only during a good flood tide, and sharing the poling and gunning duties with a shooting buddy, or in hiring a good rail bird hunting guide, who knows the migration and areas where to find them at different weeks of each month, because they are on the water and keep up with the migration. Friends if you are going to learn this sport, and learn it well, take the time to get the right gear to do it properly, and enjoy hunting in the traditional manner of rail bird hunting.

Look closely at the mathematics with regard to rail bird hunting conditions at times when a hard cold front starts pushing through, and you're out in a flooded salt marsh when the winds might be pushing your light skiff at speeds in of 3–7 knots across the flats. That, my friend, is a whole lot of ballistics to factor inside any gunner's head, before a snap shot on a jumping rail bird that's twenty yards out from the gunner's chair.

Do you question me? I think not. What is ballistics, some of you may ask? You've just got to experience rail bird hunting for yourself. However, if you're wondering what ballistics are, I'll explain. It starts with the mathematics of the gunner sighting their target, verses the elements, times the speed of the rail bird, and factors in all the distance. Multiply that by the speed of the skiff being poled—remember, you are being affected by some serious winds—and you've just got to figure it all out and put it all together before you swing onto your target and head out rail bird hunting.

Here is Joe Guide's rail bird hunting rule# 1: If it's really windy, you might consider bringing one more box of shells than you think you'll need. I will suspend my 12ga rule and allow twelve-gauge shotguns into the skiff only during really windy days, as most fellows need all the help they can get when there is that much wind pushing these rail birds across a marsh. Adults are notorious for getting up far in advance and leaving the juveniles (1- to 3-year-old birds) hiding in the tall grass that remains to be flooded. Those adults know what's out there, but I've seen mighty smart rail birds outmaneuver the finest and strongest push polers. When the wind is up, some of those birds will actually tack with the wind. You may find that hard to believe, but I'm telling you it is the truth, because I've seen it with my own eyes. Those adults are mighty smart, but you might just have to see em' with your own eyes to truly understand the complexity and just how smart these birds really are.

Sunrise over the Port City of Wilmington, NC (Judge Doug Sasser)

Clapper rail jumps from the marsh

CHAPTER ONE
THE HISTORY OF MARSH HEN (RAIL) HUNTING

The month of September normally begins the rail bird hunting season, although each state's migratory bird committee set the number of hunting days based on Federal guidelines for migratory bird hunting. It should be noted that the northern states that have wild rice, such as Maine, Wisconsin, or Minnesota could set an earlier date such as mid August for rail bird hunting to begin, as these birds do not stay in these particular regions of north America very long, usually by the end of the first week of September's full moon, rail birds are migrating southward; and should those state committees choose to begin in August rather than September this would certainly allow for limited opportunities to hunt rail birds in those particular states, more so than normal.

This would certainly allow more rail bird hunters in the Central Flyway to take advantage of the early rail bird migrations that stay briefly in areas such as Montana's marshy Freezeout Lake, Minnesota's lakes and rivers that harbor wild rice meadows, and especially the rail bird marsh habitat that is found in the reservoirs and lakes of North Dakota and Kansas, as well as the wild rice areas off the Mississippi, and the many marshy private impoundments that border all along the Mississippi Flyway in Missouri.

I believe that Maine's five rivers- with wild rice meadows that empty into Merrymeeting Bay would greatly benefit from an early opening season on rail birds in August, if it was timed to begin during that month's high tides. The other southern and northeastern states should keep their September opening timeframe, as many birds did not start arriving in local marshes until just prior to and during the full moon week each September.

Blackwood's Outdoor's Magazine ran an article called "Hunting Rail Birds" by a sportsman from New York City in 1853. Additional desirability as an early September gentleman's sport, and other articles that were written about this sporting bird, helped to make quite popular. All the major cities and the new transportation accessible to gentlemen sportsmen allowed them to do more shooting, just a short train ride from the major cities of the Northeast. Sora rail became a game bird of excellent table fare. Nevertheless, it did not grow into a nationally recognized sporting game bird until well into the 1870s, when a greater number of wealthy Northerners moved down south and started owning coastal plantations in the low country. These "gentleman sportsmen" really pursued the noble rail, hiring watermen guides who would pole handmade wooden shallow draft skiffs with greater veracity along the Atlantic Seaboard's inshore waters.

Audubon commented in his personal journals regarding the South Atlantic salt marshes how "…very few hunters pursued this particular species of marsh hen or rail bird either in the fresh or the salt waters due to the difficulty of getting to them, deep within their marsh kingdom." Audubon called the Rallidae a "noble" and "clever" marsh bird, which could easily elude man and dog. The saying "as thin as a rail" refers directly to how easily these species can filter through the marsh grass and disappear.

Maurice River NJ premier Sora rail bird–Wild rice meadows (D. White 2009)

Rail birds are still the most misunderstood of any other migratory fowl in the marshes. Of course, one can hunt railbirds in the same areas where you would hunt other waterfowl later in the season—along the coastal inshore waters, in rice meadows, off creeks, and marsh cuts, and wild rice meadows, and Spartina grass flats. It comes as a great shock to the neophyte rail hunter that rail birds are most excellent divers and swimmers. In the months of late October through December, rails seem to prefer swimming to flying. They have developed very strong legs, and although webless, they are very strong swimmers too. Early in the months of September and October, juvenile rail of all species tend to jump and fly more quickly, but they wise up as the cold fronts of October to December push hundreds of thousands, or perhaps millions of new birds southward.

As September marks the opening of Clapper rail and Sora rail bird hunting along the Atlantic Flyway, there is no doubt whatsoever that the full moon denotes the highest of flood tides Once you experience a traditional marsh hen hunt during an exceptionally high tide, in a full or new moon period, you will most assuredly become a fan of the rail bird, or "marsh hen," which is the more colloquial name of all species of rails throughout the south Atlantic. In the Northeast inshore marshes, during the September and October flood tides, the few professional guides are typically booked solid by August as established customers from Boston to New York return again and again for traditional rail bird hunts. I have customers from New York City to Hollywood that travel to Wilmington, North Carolina, to hunt rail birds with me during our highest flood tide days and a majority of these gentlemen shoot some mighty beautiful and classic shotguns.

We are now well into the twenty-first century, and we continue to read each and every year in editorials and outdoor magazines about the increasing environmental issues that impact wildfowl of all species. With the number of young waterfowlers continuing to grow throughout every flyway in North America, we will no doubt see a future of heavy hunting pressure on all species of waterfowl. Of course, as any waterfowl biologist will tell you, marsh birds such as the Rallidae are not classified as waterfowl, and their populations across our nation are certainly healthy, and have been so for more than a century. This has been due, primarily to the difficulty of hunters getting out to the marshes where rail birds are located. Although sporting gentlemen of my day, and since the 1830s never had a problem with hard work, and difficult tasks in hunting rail birds, it certainly appears that the modern day wildfowler, doesn't care to take up the push pole and obtain a light skiff, and get out into the marshes and do some scouting and hunt rails with as much determination as they would pursue other huntable species, such as ducks and geese. However, rails are indeed part of the wildfowl community and are migratory, moving down after severe cold fronts in October and November each and every year.

What I find absolutely amazing is that, if you asked one hundred people at your local DU or Delta Waterfowl banquet whether they had made the effort to hunt rail birds in the past year, you would probably find that 80% had never hunted rails in their lifetime! Rail hunters throughout the Northeast and South Atlantic coastal marshes would like to keep it that way, and not have a lot of competition in their home marshes. However, when you think about just how many thousands of miles of salt marsh there is along the Atlantic Coast, and that on average less than 300 to 600 hunters have hunted rail birds along each state in the Atlantic Flyway—when there are perhaps 5.8 million waterfowl hunters across our nation—that is quite astonishing. Most of those few hundred rail bird hunters normally hunt rail birds during only a few very high flood tides every year. This illustrates just how many millions of rail birds are out there along the Atlantic Flyway, and how few wildfowl hunters actually pursue them.

Rail bird hunting is a difficult sport, in that the hunters must pole or paddle their boats or skiffs into gunning positions. That is mighty hard work for most people to do. When some unscrupulous sportsmen try to bend the rules to fill their bag limits, the game warden is watching from a distance and will burn them—in the pocketbook and in the courtroom.

SC DNR Game Warden Major Ben Moise told me that he could average approximately 30 to 75 violation tickets to rail bird hunters each season, depending on which area of the coast he was working, and most of those were for "running and gunning"—taking rail birds while running the motor. He was one tough game warden…he even gave his own mama a ticket for fishing on a pier without a fishing license while she was visiting Charleston. One day, ol' Ben ticked thirty rail hunters and their boats for that particular violation around the John's Island marshes of South Carolina on a high tide day in the 1970s. You can read all about it in his wonderful book, *Adventures of a Low Country Game Warden* (University of South Carolina Press).

The truth is closer to those who have hunted rail for years, and who asked me to please not tell other waterfowlers about all the excitement and superb gunning for rail all along the Atlantic Flyway, which is where the largest numbers of marsh hens have been hunted since colonial days. The old-school wildfowlers have a "fear" of increased competition along the local coastal fresh water and salt water public marshes.

I believe that a good reason that rail hunters are so few in numbers could be something quite different. It could be simply that traditional rail hunting is still quite a "gentleman's sport," and it takes a great deal of hard work of poling the marsh during an incoming and full tidal period. A great number of waterfowlers are just not willing to work very hard at gunning rail birds.

There are literally over a hundred species of rail around the world. However, in North America we have just six species. Four species are huntable in America. Largest to smallest, these are the King, Clapper and Virginia rails, and the little Sora. Most watermen rarely see the smaller yellow and black or red-striped rail birds; and I have been hunting marsh hens since 1968, and I have seen only four yellow rails, two black rails, and just one red-Striped rail bird in all those years. The hard truth is that most hunters or watermen will rarely notice the yellow, or the red-striped, or the black rails. The sturdy little Sora, along with the King, are found more often in fresh water marshes, rather than the salt marshes throughout the Atlantic and Gulf Coast inshore.

In my forty-four years of gunning rail birds, 90 percent of my hunting has been along the Atlantic Flyway. I saw more Sora (Carolina rail) in the month of September 2013, than I'd ever seen in previous years. Clapper rails are the most abundant of all the coastal marsh species of rail birds. In the spring flood tides of April and May, I have literally seen thousands and thousands of rail birds and their young when doing rail bird counts off the North Carolina coastal salt marsh.

I believe that the Sora rail gets "marsh fever" and migrates early, joining only occasionally with their larger cousin, the Clapper rail, and moving southward. They will often bypass the main marshes and drop down along the lower Connecticut river rice meadows and marshes, then will move on to the New Jersey wild rice meadows, especially the two dominant meadows found along the Maurice and the Walking Rivers. A greater number remain in the south, due perhaps to the warmer winter months in the more temperate climate of the South Atlantic marshes, in order to rear their young in the months of February and March.

Perhaps Hurricane Sandy in October 2012 scared larger numbers of Rallidae southward, and they like the weather down south better. I don't see as many Soras in the salt marshes of South Carolina and Georgia, as I do the Clapper and Virginia rail. However, with less rice being planted along the fresh water rivers of the south, that is reason enough to drive the Sora more toward the coastal inshore marshes.

In the coastal marshes of Maine, Connecticut, and New Jersey, rail hunting is still being enjoyed year after year during the high tide periods of September through October. Rallidae are often referred to as "rail birds" by the locals of these northern inshore waters, and they call their fresh water rice fields, and Saltmarsh spartina grass flats 'meadows'. Although you can find some Sora rail in the coastal marshes of Virginia, North Carolina, South Carolina, and Georgia, most hunters tend to see more Clappers and, to a lesser extent, Virginia rail in the inland saltmarshes which is due to salinity issues, and primary food sources and migratory behavior, etc. Whereas in brackish water marshes you can find the Sora and King rail which both prefer less salinity.

In the Carolina low country, we bake Soras into "peep pies." Know that those little birdies can be faster fliers than most Clapper, King or Virginia rail—who are larger and stronger, albeit more awkward fliers, than their little cousin from up north—once these species jump from the marsh and take flight.

Today, with bag limits and seasons being reduced for other species of wildfowl, we rail hunters are allowed a reasonably long (70-day) season on rail. What is amazing is that for the past ten to twenty years, we have seen a daily limit of 15 Clapper/Virginia rails, and a exceptionally large bag limit of 25 Soras, which are the smallest of the rail family that most hunters will see in large numbers in fresh water tidal marshes, along with the elusive King rail. These two species can be found throughout the Atlantic's fresh and brackish water marshes, where Soras and Kings love feeding in rice fields. However, they can occasionally be found in saltmarshes where the salinity levels are not extreme. The King can also be found in the Mississippi, Central, and Western flyways, but does not linger too long in the rice fields and marshes due to the weather and the migratory movement of this species.

I was stationed in Missouri for six months back in 2003, and was surprised to find excellent Sora rail hunting in the fresh water marshes off Ol' Miss from Columbia southward to Cape Girardeau, where there are a lots of rice fields and impoundments. All the way southward along the Mississippi through the famous Stuttgart AR, you'll find

plenty of rice fields, and some marshes along the Mississippi Delta where you can shoot rail birds on their southern migrations all the way down to Louisiana, and even west of Lake Charles into Texas' salt marshes. However, I've found that most waterfowlers along the Gulf of Mexico saltmarshes do not bother with the difficulties of rail bird hunting throughout their regions. There is some rail bird hunting during the full moon tides of September and October in Mobile Bay marshes, however, it appears to that most wildfowlers don't care to do the hard work when it comes to rail bird hunting. It is really a lot of hard work in many areas and marshes not dominated by high tides, and not a lot of wildfowlers down in Alabama, Louisiana, and coastal Texas that have access to flooded rice fields where rail bird shooting could be easier to push through with a light rail bird boat, or MoMarsh type of shallow water boat you might see in tidewater marshes on the Atlantic Flyway. Those that do have hunting access to these private rice fields and impoundments in this part of the Mississippi Flyway, are more interested in dove and teal seasons, rather than searching for rail birds during their migration periods of September and October.

Along the Mississippi Delta, I've hunted the marshes along Sharkey Country to the southeast Louisiana marshes—and really, those coastal areas are just are not conducive to hunting rail birds. The tides are not high enough to flood those marshes, except during serious storms, and you really don't want to get into that mix. Of the entire Gulf, you'll need to concentrate on the Mobile Delta, the Mississippi Delta, and some areas along southeast Louisiana if you are really interested in hunting rail birds down there in October and early November, as seasons and conditions allow you to pursue them in those areas.

In Washington, Oregon, and California, the Pacific Flyway—rail birds migrate early from their Canadian marshes, where they breed. Few wildfowlers in the Pacific Delta marshes have ever hunted them and most articles tend to be environmental in nature are often written on the endangered California King Rail bird. This particular rail bird has been a protected species for some time now, with efforts being made by CDNR to save that species from extension. As you can imagine, the Sacramento Delta Marsh and its marsh habitat has been devastated due to real estate encroachment and environmental runoff into the bay.

The California rail used to be hunted around fresh water marshes in eastern Oregon, and in the old Tule Lake marshes in Northern California, and in the Sacramento Delta marshes, from the late 1870s to the 1950s. San Francisco Bay's marshes, as well as the Sacramento Valley rice fields, used to have them in large numbers by the full moon of October. In the 1920s – WWII years there were perhaps four hundred or more hunters pursuing rail birds in the marsh regions of California, however by the 1950s and early sixties there were fewer than one hundred and fifty too few to ever pressure that rail species. It was the onslaught of urban development, through its steady encroachment with pollution runoff into the coastal delta marshes over the years, which caused a deadly impact in those coastal salt marsh regions. I believe that large 501 (c)3 nonprofit organizations such as Ducks Unlimited need to do more in this flyway to study the CKR, and rail bird hunting in general. I know individuals that struggle to donate $25 or $50 a year to DU, and have other friends who think nothing of giving $10,000 annually to DU or Delta Waterfowl. I think that marsh birds such as the rail bird give us a great insight into migratory healthiness within salt and freshwater marsh bird communities, and there needs to be more research and banding studies by both our USFW bird banding studies as well as the larger Wildfowl organizations that I have mentioned.

JP Hand pushing rail hunter-Merrymeeting Bay, ME. Oct 2011

Dr. Ron is ready for action

Our youth are the future of wildfowling in America

CHAPTER TWO
THE ATLANTIC FLYWAY

There are rich and full histories of rail hunting along the marshes from Merrymeeting Bay in Maine. Wildfowlers in other flyways across the nation have heard about the thousands of acres of wild rice around the Mississippi Flyway and along that great river. Many readers may be aware that Missouri and Arkansas, as well the central flyway states of Wisconsin and Minnesota has thousands and thousands of acres of wild rice growing along rivers and lakes, and far west in the Pacific Flyway's California saltmarshes and Sacramento flooded rice field impoundments in northern California, rail hunting is not allowed, due to the endangered California King rail bird.

In the state of Maine, wild rice abounds in thousands of acres along the edges the big bay and its five rivers that flow into Merrymeeting Bay. There are still hearty souls who pole handmade wooden skiffs rail bird hunting in September. Their season for rail bird hunting is quite short due to the weather and the rail bird migration. This is the outdoor world of L.L. Bean, that great outdoorsman of years ago who had a cabin in sight of that bay.

In the Atlantic Flyway, where rail hunting is still the traditional sport of gentlemen, hunters shoot from a chair secured in the forward section of a rail boat. That boat is pushed by a guide, poling the craft during the highest of tides, and flushing rails with their boat through the mere strength of muscle power. My friends, poling is still a craft where educated guides with strong backs and keen minds are hard to find today.

In the 1880s along these northeastern marshes, wherever one might have been hunting rail back then—Merrymeeting Bay's marshes, or along the Maurice River in the southeastern New Jersey rice field marshes, or way up the Connecticut River rice fields—good guides received perhaps five dollars for poling a gentleman rail gunner to shoot their 25 to 50 Sora rails in a 1 ½ to 2 ½ hour time period, depending on the tide and region. In many families of watermen, they guided and poled generations of wealthy and middle-class sportsmen from New York, New Jersey, Philadelphia, and Boston, who took the train or ship (and sometime both) to those coastal hunting communities for the sport of rail hunting every September and October.

Down south, a good poler was lucky to get a couple of dollars for three hours of poling around a marsh after rails, commonly called marsh hens. Wealthy industrialists who purchased plantations following the Reconstruction Period after the Civil War took up rail hunting, as they did along the Connecticut, Delaware, Maryland, the Virginias', and the Carolinas' coastal salt marshes and former rice fields. Southern gentlemen who hunted waterfowl got into rail hunting, which had been ignored for table fare due to the smallness of these marsh birds. However, rail bird hunting picked up several enthusiasts throughout the coastal communities south of Savanna, Georgia, as well as those marshes down from St. Simons Island, around the Brunswick Islands, and even down in the northeastern Florida marshes off Amelia Island and west of Fernanda.

Rail birds are migratory. The federal agencies that determine the bags and seasons of waterfowl hunting are responsible for our rail seasons and bag limits as well. However, they do not offer much financial assistance to study these unique species, except on very limited banding studies in 1965 and 1971 to determine whether the Clapper and Sora rail bird numbers were decreasing or increasing.

There is an annual spring marsh bird forecast done each and every year. Most of the volunteers that study marsh birds, such as rails, do not have the shallow water boats to do much more than set up recording devices in creeks and cuts near marshes and rice fields along the coast. Some researchers do set up a number of safety traps to trap study these marsh birds, like the rail. However, there is much more than can be done if more financial effort is made by the federal agencies.

The powers that be cite hunting pressure from reports gathered from DNR Hunting records of wildfowl and HIP statistical analysis from Maine through Texas. There is little pressure from hunters, but waterfowl biologists are more fearful of encroachment by real estate development upon the coastal wetlands than hunters. A 1965 banding study showed this data: a Clapper Rail, 7 years and 4 month old, banded 8/11/1963 in Florida (local banding) was shot and recovered 10/16/1976 in Florida. There was a Clapper rail, 7 years and 6 months old, banded 5/24/1971 in New Jersey (after the hatching year), shot and recovered from the Jersey saltmarshes on 12/05/1977.

In 2007, there were 1,500 rail bird hunters who notified HIP that they hunted rail birds in South Carolina that season. However, there must be more definitive rail bird studies than a HIP which often is rush through in preparation of obtaining a new hunting licence, this is noted by statistical discrepancies such as there were less than 150 hunters in 2008 who pursued rail birds in South Carolina, and less than 120 hunters recorded that they hunted rail in 2009 through 2010. Less than 50 claimed in their HIP to have hunted them in Georgia during those years, and less than 27 in Florida listed hunting rails on their HIP report.

In the great North Eastern region of our Nation, the state of Maine accounted for < 45 hunting rail, and Connecticut DNR reported less than 100 rail hunters in 2008 – 2010 season's HIP reports. Yet the New Jersey coastal town of Morristown still remains one of the great rail hunting regions of the northeastern United States. Morristown has been the northeastern Mecca for Sora rail bird shooting in the United States from 1940s to 1970s.

Well over 5,000 hunters came there annually to hunt rail birds in southern New Jersey's wild rice meadows, and to be pushed by local guides, or well known watermen like Mr. John Bradford of Buckshutem, Cumberland County, N.J., who knew the Delaware marshes and bays and wild rice meadows and rivers. He like others guides grew up nearby and fished and hunted their home marshes and waters, and loved everything about the sport. The more difficult the poling in standing wild rice, the better for those few and hardy souls who made up the rail bird hunting guides of that day and time. They earned their pay, and built their skiffs and push poles and prided themselves and their knowledge and of keeping up where the best rail bird hunting was located for their "sports".

Traditionally, guides during the Great Depression years received $5 or $10 for about three hours of poling, which was certainly excellent money for that time period, and needed income for families of watermen, which increased over the years. The Great Depression cut back almost all but the wealthiest of bird hunters, and sustenance hunting of many wildfowl increased. However, it did not negatively impact rail bird hunting except those along the sea island marshes that feasted on rail bird eggs, and "going egging" was a popular youth activity that decimated the breeding population of clapper rail bird nests in early spring's nesting season in those coastal marshes.

There are the Camp's from southern New Jersey, who got into guiding during the WWII years, and whose name is linked with the Maurice River. Members of Walter Camp's family of rail bird hunters continue to use their historic two man railbird skiffs, some well over sixty years old, and their stories handed down from a couple of generations of that family and other hunting families are important to the township of Mauricetown, New Jersey.

Guides' fees increased with the times, like everything else, depending on where you lived and hunted. By the early 1960s, it could cost you as much as $100 to hire a rail bird guides to push you for one tide. In the 1980s, rail bird guide fees were running around $200 to $250 a person, and by the late 1990s it was around $300 to $350 per person. The best and brightest rail bird guides are booked up very early, as there are perhaps three or four exceptional high tides each lunar week, and during every month. So you might have only eight excellent flood tides each month, and all good guides have repeat customers, such as fathers and sons embarking on a traditional rail bird hunt each year for generations.

New wildfowl hunters get introduced to this sport, and today's top rail bird guides command approximately $350 to $500 for a "flood tide period" of gunning. That includes your round-trip travel time, from the boat landing to the hunting area along the miles and miles of wild rice meadows or salt marsh flats, during the high flood tidal periods during September and October—or until a massive storm or cold front hits that region, and the rail birds take wing for the southern coastal marshes of the southeastern Atlantic Flyway. In southern states like Virginia and North Carolina, seasons run from September until November; and in South Carolina, Georgia, and Florida, seasons can be split and run until the last flood tide in December.

Breeding is a spring thing, and as seasons continue to be warmer and warmer, more Clapper rail, Virginia, and some King rail birds are becoming residents and staying in the south, rather than going northward to Saskatchewan's Quill Lake, and Cumberland marshes, or Manitoba and Hudson Bay's marshes, and the vast Sitanok Marshes as well as the Canadian Maritime marshes in the spring months, just to return each fall once again and go through their circle of migration life. Without more banding data, and research funding for sora and clapper rail birds which are the two dominate species one really doesn't get a clear idea of just how many rail birds migrate through the Central and Mississippi Flyways of North America.

Not so the little Sora rail bird. They are strong migrators, and each spring move northward, always at night and especially during the full moon weeks. I have interviewed watermen who have seen and heard the migration of hundreds or thousands of Sora rail birds coming in during the nights of the full moon, in such numbers that are simply amazing to imagine. Some nights they come in flocks of hundreds, and sometime thousands of railbirds, where just the day prior there were quite few seen or heard in the wild rice meadows. This, of course, has been happening each fall and spring with the migratory species across our great nation, before it was even considered to be a British colony. Migratory wildfowl have always been moving above the heads of the commoner and those in high colonial office alike, throughout the seasons of the year. God willing, the migratory patterns of the rail bird shall always continue that cycle as it always has throughout the ages along the greatest of the flyways, and the most ancient is the Atlantic Flyway which is the greatest flyway for rail bird hunting in the United States of America.

Bob White has some tough poling through this marsh

1979, Jamie waits for a VA Rail to jump from the marsh.

CHAPTER THREE
RAIL BOATS, MOTORS, & PUSH POLES

There are a lot of Old School rail bird hunters in the northeastern states that really enjoy using hand-built wooden rail bird skiffs and pushing through the region's freshwater rice meadows. When the tide starts dropping, we need to get our light, shallow water rail boats or skiffs out of the marsh as quickly as possible. Not all boats have motors or jack plates that can allow you to quickly get a "hole shot," and to get that particular boat "on plane." With these, you could then get off a flat very fast, especially when you really need to get out of an area with a falling tide.

Look closely at the different types of rail boats used for different types of flats. You will see a number of different rail hunting boats in this chapter. Take a good look at them, notice their lines, and think about shooting from some of the boats. You will quickly see that the northeastern freshwater rivers with thick, wild rice meadows necessitate the need for a light, small, pointy skiff that can push through wild rice. My word, you may have thought in looking at some of the photos of rail bird hunting in heavy rice, how can people see to shoot at rail birds in such cover, and how can they find the Sora or Virginia rail that are found in the flooded wild rice fields?

In the northeastern regions of our nation, and of course in a number of lakes and rivers in the state of Minnesota, you will find during the migration of the Sora rail bird that thousands or hundreds of thousands descend upon rice fields. Where wild rice is naturally grown, it can normally be mighty thick and tall. You can only get into it during the highest of a high tide…and then for just a limited time, if it's tidal controlled. Some hunters strongly believe in using "throwing colorful markers" when hunting in heavy rice in order to find a higher percentage of downed Soras in the flats or meadows. The additional duties of the poler/pusher, be it guide or partner, are to sight the bird, give direction, sight the kill, and "toss a marker" as close as possible to the downed bird. That method works, but it's not necessary in the southeast, because it can be much easier to find downed birds if you are hunting in short Spartina grass, or if the flood tide is mighty high and completely covering the grass, or if you are using a good retrieving dog.

I will talk more about retrievers, and specific dogs that are best suited for rail bird hunting, in that particular section of this book. Suffice it to say that no dog can properly retrieve rail birds in heavy wild rice, as it's certainly too hard and harsh an environment to work a retriever, and the rice is so thick that until it's beaten down, it is not conducive for retrievers. It can be mighty tough to simply push through it at times, even with a light wooden rail boat skiff that might weigh around 150 pounds. That is something to think about—just look at some of the photos of rail boats pushing through various wild rice meadows in the boat section of this book, and you can see for yourself just how heavy these meadows are in the Northeast or Wisconsin, Minnesota, or southern Illinois.

BIG SKIFFS...LITTLE RAIL BOAT SKIFFS

Every so often, I see some of the big ol' technical flat boats and skiffs that some guides are using today. You've seen them in magazines, with sleek lines and large outboards. These manufactured flats boats may draft as much as 6 to 12 inches depending on their design, as well as engine type and weight capabilities when fully loaded. Large technical skiffs such as the Hewes Craft, Hells Bay, Action Craft, Southern Skimmer, Carolina Skiff, and Parker Brothers Skiffs, will draft just too much, in my professional opinion. They are just too heavy a boat to be used along the southeast coastal saltmarshes for rail bird hunting, except for a limited time during the highest of high tides,

However, there are a handful of lighter technical skiffs on the market, such as the Beavertail, Mitzi, and the Ranger Ghost, to name a few. These are truly light, and may draft closer to 6 inches. Light technical skiffs could be used if their owners desire to go rail bird hunting in some of the Maryland, Virginia, North Carolina, South Carolina, Georgia, and Florida salt marsh Spartina grass flats that experience 5.4 – 8.0> foot high tides during September, October, and November. The higher tides listed are found on the Georgia coast.

Now, you could of course use your larger flats boats to carry or tow in a small, light rail boat or skiff into a position upwind of a particular flat. This is useful if it's some distance to travel on the water from the landing to the particular flats where you may be hunting rail birds. Get a good tide chart, study it, and see how well it matches up. There are many different charts out on the market. Look at the differences listed on a couple of these charts before you trust one in the area you're going to hunt.

You will notice one of the photos from Maine's Merrymeeting Bay where there is a large, motorized canoe towing a single rail boat across a large body of water to a particular wild rice meadow where they planned to pole and hunt. In the 1960s and '70s, we used to pull our wooden rail boats from the landing a few miles down the ICW to the flats we were going to pole, and might have another person in the motorboat- who would run it down the ICW to the end of the large salt marsh flat in order to (a) pick up and tow us back to the landing after we got to the far side, or (b) tow our skiff to another flat, if there was enough time to get to a second flat while the tide was still flooding.

Of course, you should realize that these large, technical flats boats are really made for crossing large bodies of water, and for technical poling once you've arrived on a particular flat with a flood tide that is high and safe enough for you to pole that particular craft across. You've just got to use common sense, check the flats with your pole or paddle, and remember the tide chart for that area on that particular day.

I would like to point out that there are many large Jon boats on the market that draft < 4 inches. However, there are only a few that will draft in less than 3 inches with three people. I designed my 19' x 69" D3 Marsh Master Skiff (see photo), which was specially made for poling in skinny water, and is a dream to pole in any salt marsh from Maryland south through the Carolinas, Georgia and Florida, and the Gulf of Mexico's inshore waters.

Keep in mind that down along the Gulf of Mexico, there are just not enough very high tides, unless heavy winds are pushing water against a flat and pushing the tide table accordingly. Normally there is not enough flood tide along the Gulf coasts to float any heavy technical skiff. In western Florida, Alabama, Louisiana, or Texas where rail birds might winter, there are of course some reservoirs and impoundments where you might find some Sora rails migrating or feeding into, or some marsh lands on private impoundments. Here you can usually get around in a kayak, canoe, light Jon boat, or something like those Missouri MOMARSH light skiffs, to do some gunning on rails.

However, most of the most gulf tides are just not high enough to flood most of their salt marsh grass flats. You cannot use larger flats boats, because most of 'em are just too heavy, and draft greater than 6 inches. Those technical flats skiffs just cannot get in and out of Spartina grass flats with any confidence, but they are used on the Georgia coasts when the flood tides of September and October run > 8 feet, and I have seen some technical skiff used down in Virginia's Back Bay, and out in Chincoteague whenever the heavy flood tides push water back into Spartina alterniflora flats each fall.

In the fall months, I've seen Jon boats, and wooden rail bird boats pushing through the Spartina marshes rail bird hunting off Currituck, South River, and North River marshes of North Carolina, the Middle Marshes off Beaufort, North Carolina, and the Cape Fear, as well as down southern low country marshes off Winyah Bay, and Debidue Plantation near Georgetown, S.C., and down around James Island and off the Ashley, Cooper and Wando Rivers off Charleston, as well as the ACE Basin down off Beaufort, South Carolina coasts when the high tides run in greater than 6.4. But you could push up and along some of the creeks, and pound the grass points with your push pole.

Any fly fisherman who fishes who poles their skiff into any of these marsh areas during the breeding season each spring's high tide periods will see more Clapper rail bird clutches especially during the flood tides of April and realize just how many marsh hens are really in their marshes. Those bird sightings are more relevant than the Audubon bird counts of rail birds which are done during the "Christmas bird counts," however these historical bird counts by members of the Audubon Society are relevant, yet limited in scope due to the time period, however it is still a matter of record that will tell a story in itself, but not the whole story of how healthy the Clapper and Sora rail bird is especially in the Atlantic Flyway today.

These are first hand personal views of Clapper populations each spring in the Spartina grass flats from Virginia throughout the Carolinas, Georgia to the NE Coast of Florida and I am a much better judge of the Sora and Clapper rail populations than Sauer 2007 study which felt that all species were in decline. You cannot simply base your studies on a couple of Waterfowl Biologists' call analysis, or rail bird track analysis, or the Audubon Christmas Counts, but you can from watermen and wildfowlers who hunt, and fish and travel and visit saltmarshes at various seasons of the year and observe these species and keep records and journals.

No matter what state I'm hunting rail birds in, there will be hunters who love to hunt the rail birds and are always reluctant to leave a flat, especially when they are enjoying themselves, and sometimes get stuck when the tide drops off the flat quickly. You may have been out during a "super tide" during September or October, or some exceptional high tides found in the new moon or full moon periods of November and December along the South Atlantic states, and perhaps you were not watching the water table drop. Or perhaps the winds were pushing the water and increasing the lunar tidal heights, but suddenly those winds are no longer blowing quite as strong, or perhaps the wind switched directions—and you realize that you've got to get out of there quickly and get to deeper water, or you'll find yourself grounded!

If you don't have a light skiff, a light Jon boat, or a special rail boat, you might very well find yourself stuck. You might have to wait seven or eight hours for the tides to return, in order to get your heavier boat out of that flat. So learn to read the tides and the winds, as well as your distance from a deep exit point, anytime you are poling across a rail bird flat or wild rice meadow—no matter what type of rail bird hunting boat you're using.

Be smart, be safe, and have a boating plan to cover a particular distance of poling. Set your watch alarm with enough time to get out of a flooded flat with your rig, and follow your hunt safety plan. If the winds are blowing and pushing water, stacking it up higher in a particular flat that you happen to be hunting, then realize you may have a little more time. If you are lucky, it could extend the tidal height from +/- 30 minutes to close to an extra hour over your printed tide chart. You've just got to learn how to judge these conditions and tides over time, and hopefully not get stranded out in a flat because you waited too long to chase rail birds around a particular flooded flat that is suddenly falling off quicker than expected.

Be observant of the tide levels, and agree with your boat mates regarding when you need to get off the water. Unless, of course, you have a guide who knows the area, and knows exactly how much time you can stay in a flat or rice meadow before the tide drops precipitously.

Clapper, King, VA, and Sora Rail birds in 2013 bag –Joe Guide Photo

Gunner resting in a skiff

Shawn Bennet tries to walk up a clapper in the falling tide

Dr. Phil tries to jump a Clapper out of the Brunswick Coastal Spartina grass

CHAPTER FOUR
SHOTGUNS, SHELLS, & ACCESORIES

There is no doubt in my mind that most wildfowlers will not use a twelve gauge shotgun to hunt rail birds, except in very heavy winds, and with the lightest of non-toxic loads. One should always consider the proper shotgun in gunning a particular species.

I prefer the traditional side-by-side shotgun, and occasionally use an O/U. However, I will carry an old but sturdy .410 SXS in pursuit of marsh hens. I shoot a lot of skeet with that same .410 double barrel with beavertail forearm, 30" barrels, and double triggers. Normally I will average 23 out of 25, when I'm on the skeet range. My average shot at rails will rarely exceed 25 yards.

I recommend various gauges of shotguns for rail bird hunting, especially a .410, 20ga, or 28 or 16 ga shotguns, and recommend low brass #6 or # 7 ½ non-toxic or steel is sufficient- depending on what my clients are more comfortable shooting.

I don't feel it relevant to use a 12-gauge shotgun for hunting rail birds, except when it's really windy, as it's just too much gun for this species, unless you use low brass non toxic or steel# 7 ½ shot. Of course, there are occasions—especially on very windy days when the wind speed is greater than 18 knots—that it's necessary to use a 20ga shot gun, or even a 28ga if you have one. However, most days a 20-gauge with # 7 ½ shot will suffice when seated in the front gunner's chair in all winds and conditions.

Shell selection. I always recommend using non-toxic shot, even if you are hunting in a state that still allows lead. To me, it is an environmental issue. Rails, like doves and snipe, are migratory birds. However, each of the rail species are unique web-less marsh birds, and therefore are not classified as waterfowl. Although marsh birds are indeed wildfowl that breed and migrate via fresh and salt water, some rail species, such as the Sora and King, do prefer fresh water over salt. These two species certainly love feeding in rice fields, but first and foremost, all rail birds are classified as marsh birds.

Waterfowlers across the country and the world would certainly realize why the U.S. recommended, beginning in the late 1970s, that hunters of waterfowl use only non-toxic shot hunting ducks, geese and swan. It was due to lead poisoning cases, outlined in studies from waterfowl biologists and other researchers. Using non-toxic shot while rail hunting, even if your home state still allows lead shot for rail, is just the right environmental thing to do.

Therefore, wherever I am hunting, and anytime you hunt in my skinny water skiff, you are going to use only non-toxic shot for rail hunting. These are the same areas one would hunt waterfowl, and only non-toxic shot is used for them. I personally recommend Winchester Super X steel, or Federal Steel # 6 or #7 shotgun shells for all marsh hens. A lot of my guests hunt with other exotic and more costly non-toxic shells, such as bismuth, but those shells and the older wildfowl shotguns used by many today are much more expensive. Some of these non-toxic shot shells are more costly than steel, but easier on most of the older shotguns enjoyed by many wildfowlers today.

Being an old-school wildfowler at heart, I certainly love to shoot the classic side-by-side (SxS) shotguns in .410 or 20ga. I do see a lot of my clients using primarily side-by-side or over-and-under shotguns, and appreciate the quality of their craftsmanship and care. I see many rail bird hunters use bismuth non-toxic shot in their older classic shotguns, which cuts down on the high pressure loads of traditional steel shot shells.

I certainly do see a lot of guns, such as 20ga, or .410 Winchester M21 SxS, and even the Winchester M24 series SxS. I use to see a lot more of LC Smith's SxS, but not very many Fox Model-Bs, and I certainly do see a lot of older Remington Auto-20ga shotguns, Browning BSS, Citori O/U, and Beretta O/Us, as well as the sturdy and reliable Russian Baikal shotguns in 28ga, and 20ga SxS, or O/U's with 28-inch barrels. Occasionally I see some newer shotguns, but most of my clients come from New York City, New Jersey, D.C., Philadelphia, Charlotte, Raleigh, Louisiana, and Atlanta, and most clients really tend to hunt rail birds more with SxS and O/U than automatics.

An enjoyable and familiar shot gunning outing can be experienced whenever rail birds are plentiful during a flood tide early in the season, whether you are shooting an expensive Benelli or a Peruzzi, or even a Stoger O/U. However, I can also appreciate seeing clients using their father's or grandfather's Browning, Remington, or Mossberg automatic shotguns, primarily in 20ga. That third shot comes in handy when five to seven birds jump out of a clump of thick Spartina grass, as well as throughout the split season, especially after late October, when rail birds tend to gather more together after a cold front pushes down. On the highest of super flood tides, you can often find larger groups of six to ten rail birds hanging tightly together. Your practice time on the skeet or trap range will pay off tremendously.

Here is the current information regarding lead verses non-toxic shot usage in a number of states that have migratory and resident rail populations. You will note that some states are quite specific with their guidelines, and others may be open to interpretation. Always check your current state's F&G regulations with DNR or your local Game Warden.

Non-toxic shot regulations by state:

Ammunition other than lead required for "all waterfowl".

Alabama: Non-toxic shot required for migratory birds, except doves.
California: Non-toxic ammunition required in the eight-county historic range of the California condor. However, rail hunting is not currently allowed in this state due to the endangered California King rail.
Delaware: During the month of September, all hunters must use non-toxic shot when dove hunting in State Wildlife Areas. Non-toxic ammunition required for dove hunting in Wildlife Management Areas.
Illinois: Non-toxic ammunition required for dove hunting on some public lands.
Iowa: Non-toxic ammunition required for all game in wildlife management areas (except for deer and turkeys). Non-toxic ammunition is required for snipe and/or rail on all state and private land, and for grouse, quail and/or pheasant on some state land.
Kansas: Non-toxic shot required for hunting of all migratory game birds except dove and woodcock. At least 17 state wildlife areas and refuges require non-toxic shotgun load for upland game birds such as pheasant, grouse, quail, and other small game.
Kentucky: Non-toxic ammunition required for doves in 13 wildlife management areas and national wildlife refuges.
Louisiana: Non-toxic ammunition required for doves at Pointe-aux-Chenes Wildlife Management Area.
Maine: Non-toxic ammunition required in shotguns for upland game other than deer and turkey in national wildlife refuges, and in wildlife management areas and refuges, and for migratory game birds including snipe and/or rail on all state and private lands.
Maryland: Non-toxic shot is required for hunting rail and snipe.
Minnesota: Non-toxic ammunition required in the Upper Mississippi River National Wildlife Area.
Missouri: Non-toxic ammunition for shotguns required in 21 conservation areas.
Montana: Non-toxic shot required on federal national wildlife refuges and federal waterfowl production areas.
Nebraska: Non-toxic shot is required for all shotgun hunting within federal waterfowl production areas, national wildlife refuges, and some state wildlife management areas, as posted.
New Jersey: Non-toxic ammunition required for rail, snipe, or moorhens on all state and private lands.

Nevada: Non-toxic ammunition required for gallinules and snipe and in wildlife management areas.
New Mexico: Non-toxic ammunition required for common moorhen; Virginia & Sora rail; and snipe with shotguns, as well as dove, band-tailed pigeon, upland game, or migratory game birds on all State Game Commission owned or managed areas.
New York: Non-toxic ammunition required for snipe, rails or gallinules.
North Carolina: Lead allowed for rail hunting. Non-toxic shot required for the taking of migratory waterfowl and captive-reared mallards on shooting preserves, in field trials, WMA, and during bona fide dog training activities.
North Dakota: Non-toxic shot required for sand hill cranes, tundra swans, and snipe statewide, and for all shotgun hunting on all U.S. Fish and Wildlife Service lands, including federal refuges (except turkeys and big game).
Ohio: Non-toxic shot only allowed in Metzger Marsh, Mallard Club, Pipe Creek, and Magee Marsh, Toussaint, and Little Portage wildlife areas.
Oklahoma: Only non-toxic shot while hunting all species of game on the Sequoyah and Washita National Wildlife Refuge, and at Red Slough Wildlife Management Area and Hackberry Flats Wetlands.
Oregon: Non-toxic ammunition required for upland bird (i.e. non-water fowl) hunting on some national wildlife refuges and some wildlife areas.
Pennsylvania: Non-toxic ammunition required for turkey and crow.
South Carolina: Non-toxic ammunition required in some wildlife management areas (WMA).
South Dakota: Non-toxic ammunition required on most state land and U.S. military land for small game and for sand hill crane, snipe, and tundra swan.
Tennessee: Non-toxic ammunition required in some wildlife management areas and refuges.
Texas: Non-toxic shot required for all game birds in wildlife management areas and federal wildlife refuges.
Utah: Non-toxic ammunition required for sand hill crane and some wildlife management areas.
Virginia: Non-toxic ammunition required for migratory game birds: snipe, rail, moorhens, and gallinules
Washington: Non-toxic shot required in many wildlife areas, pheasant release sites, and recreation areas.
Wisconsin: Non-toxic shot required for doves on all Department of Natural Resources-managed lands and national wildlife refuges.
Wyoming: Non-toxic shot required for grouse and chukka and gray partridges on all national wildlife refuges, and chukka and gray partridges and all small game in the Springer and Table Mountain Wildlife Habitat Management Areas.

*** Note that this list may not be complete, as laws are constantly changing. Always check your local state hunting regulations each season for any updates and all current regulations.

As to other important accessories, your boat should have a good GPS, VHR radio, PDF for all hands, and if hunting in wild rice, you should carry a few colorful throwing markers to toss and mark your downed birds. Keep it simple.

Dr. Dave readies for a flush

CHAPTER FIVE
RETRIEVING DOGS

When talking about the proper use of retrieving dogs for rail bird hunting, we must look at two aspects: the area you are gunning, and both the Labrador and the Chesapeake Bay Retriever—which are by far the most popular and strongest of retrievers able to handle the heavy Spartina grass that is prevalent throughout the southeast and Gulf Coast inshore waters.

I have seen some Boykin Spaniels get pretty beat up while trying to retrieve rail birds in the heavy green Spartina grass on a hot September flood tide. Smaller dogs are mighty nice and eager. However, they will eventually tire out in heavy grass when hunting the salt marshes along the Atlantic Seaboard.

BEAR the Boykin Spaniel looks across the saltmarsh

Take a look at the photos of the different retrieving dogs listed in this section, in order to get a better perspective on the kind of flats that you are going to be hunting rail birds in during your next trip, and ask your friends or your guide what they think about you bringing your best retrieving buddy on your next rail bird hunt. I think that, due to their size; Boykin's have their place in the salt marsh like all retrieving dogs, especially during very high tides. They do okay, but you just cannot expect a 40lb Boykin to retrieve fifteen or thirty birds in heavy Spartina grass. Saltmarsh flats and spartina grass is a Lab or a Chesapeake Bay Retreaters' world, perhaps even a American Water Spaniel, but I have seen very few Golden retreaters' worth a damn in the water over the past forty years.

Chessapeake Bay retriever in flooded green Spartina grass. Thunder might retrieve as many as 150+ railbirds each season

When you are out gunning wild rice meadows in September, it's just not conducive for the use of any retrieving dogs whatsoever, and this is understandable due to the nature of just how high and thick these meadows are until the heavy rice stalks have been blown down later on in October due to strong cold fronts. Usually by that time, the larger migrations of

Sora rail birds have moved southward in late October. It's tough enough just to find 95 percent of the Sora rail birds you do kill in wild rice fields when they drop twenty yards away from the boat. Those guides who've got keen and steady eyes like a hawk are mighty rare!

Those who have never yet shot in wild rice will quickly see for yourself in the photos from Sora rail bird hunts throughout the northeastern rice meadows just how difficult it would be for retrieving dogs until the rice has been blown down, and even then it's might difficult for any but the strongest of water dogs. You've got to keep a mighty sharp eye, and that is why when gunning rail birds in wild rice throughout the Northeastern states, it's important to use throwing markers when you are poling gunners. You can see from some of the photos how even humans and boats can seem to disappear within the rice meadows, let alone the difficulty of finding the Sora railbird that you just killed. That is why some hunters use markers to mark down birds in the wild rice.

Your guide has to have eagle's eyes, and either he or you need to keep focused on exactly where your rail bird went down, and go directly to it. Also, your gunner must not be tempted to shoot another bird whenever they jump in front the skiff, when in the process of searching for and picking up a downed bird, unless that bird has been properly marked with a throwing marker. You can see some examples of throwing markers in two photos of this book, especially in the Boats section.

Here heavy grass–good dog's 30th retrieve

Retrieve

Good Shot Mr. Shawn drops a clapper (Phil Hanvey, Sept 2009 photo)

One bird short of a 15 Clapper rail bird limit, 45 min into the hunt.

CHAPTER SIX
Environmental Issues Impacting Rail Birds, Their Habitat, Breeding, and Feeding Areas, and Hunting

I wish to thank all the wildfowl and waterfowl biologists of the U.S. Fish and Wildlife Service (USFWS), and other birders and researchers who took time and effort in answering all my inquiries over the four years of my research and travel that went into the creation of *The Rail Bird Hunter's Bible*.

American sportsmen may not realize that the great majority of rail birds are produced in the Canadian marshes, are in fact actually hatched on private freshwater marshes or coastal saltmarshes, and that many are threatened by the dragline, or natural resources exploration projects; one then turns toward the 501 (c) 3 non profit mega waterfowl organizations such as DU or Delta or the Canadian refuge marshes. Of course, south of the border, the US FWS Refuge systems inshore of the Atlantic Seaboard encompass prime migratory saltwater or freshwater marshes.

JP Hand and Mr. Doug Maurice River, NJ. Sept 1989

I found all the HIP reports on rail bird hunting, small articles and personal journals, and comments from older Americans and the numbers of rail bird hunters corresponding with me over these years about hunting rail birds in Minnesota, Wisconsin, Idaho, Montana, Illinois, North Dakota, South Dakota, Kansas and Ohio river valleys, marshes, farm impoundments, and prairie pot holes, wherever this species is legally hunted.

All the personal letters, emails, and phone calls, along with the HIP reports and communication with wildfowl biologists, birders, and people interested in my research was invaluable—and most kind—in all the follow-up questions that were answered to many of my primary and secondary personal questions, research questions, and statistical research and analysis over the years of my studies of all the huntable rail bird species. I'm grateful for all the answers to my questions that came from University researchers, historians, hunters, HIP data and deeper questions to game wardens, birders, researchers, and people young and old throughout fresh and salt water marsh communities that are relevant to my studies and research.

Access to the limited number of rail bird band surveys that were currently on record, and the HIP reports of records, allowed me to study the statistical computation of birds killed by state and flyway, as well as the migration of a species. HIP surveys were studies since that data had been first recorded in the USDFW services in early 1991.

It was mighty enjoyable to converse with rail bird hunters who love to hunt marsh hens/rail birds across our nation, and all those Canadian wildfowl hunters who patiently replied to my phone calls, letters, and inquires as to their own unique experiences in pursuit of these unique species, as well as the many members of waterfowling organizations such as Ducks Unlimited and Delta Waterfowl all across our nation, who were most kind in responding to my letters, phone calls, and emails over the past four years while I traveled across the nation—hunting, mucking through marshes fresh an tidal, and researching scholarly material, research papers, and HIP data for this book.

About thirty-four years ago, while still a very young man, I wrote my friend Grits Gresham, the Outdoors writer, a series of personal letters. In one of them, I remarked that I "…hoped to write one wildfowl hunting book about a species, and make it the most scholarly wildfowl book in North America." He wished me well in that endeavor, and thanked me once again for inviting him to the South Carolina coast to hunt rail birds and other wildfowl. However, he was never able to make that trip.

I have had the great pleasure of meeting with many captains of industry, gentlemen and women, and Hollywood celebrities, and had the pleasure of getting them better educated about the excellent gunning of Clapper, Sora, and Virginia rail throughout the high tidal periods of September through December in the South Carolina season; and the September through November season in North Carolina. I've enjoyed gunning them while stationed in Maryland, Virginia, the Carolinas, Georgia, and Florida.

In the Central and Mississippi Flyways, I've hunted railbirds in Mississippi, Alabama, LA and Texas. I've looked for them in the marshes of Western Washington State and in Southern Oregon and Northern CA marshes during September and October and during bird counts in the nesting period in the spring months. I searched for the elusive California King rail with friends in the Wilson Society, and the Audubon Society while we were knee deep in the marshes around San Francisco, and traveled with my spotting scope to the rice fields of the Sacramento Delta farms looking for other rail birds during some weekends of September and October 2011 while I was a DRMI student at the Naval Post Graduate School.

In that same light, I've been quite frustrated at not finding a great number of rail birds when seeking them along northwest Florida's fresh water delta marshes, as well as in Alabama and Mississippi Valley marshes. I found Sora, and Clapper, but no Atlantic King, or Virginia rails.

I found a number of rail birds in six parishes of Louisiana, but not in northwest or southwest Missouri, though there are migrating Sora along the Eastern fresh water rice fields and marshes. I found very few numbers throughout the Texas Tropical rail along the Gulf Coast's salt marshes, but I did find them in flooded freshwater impoundments, and along New Mexico's Rio Grande watershed marshes, and Arizona's Colorado River watershed. I searched for them in Alberta, and found some rail birds in southern Saskatchewan in early September, as well as in Manitoba, Ontario, in the Maritime marshes. While stationed in California, I searched for rails from the Salton Sea to the Sacramento Delta marshes, and was finally successful in finding a few California King rails after searching many diverse, marshy areas of the Great Bear State, primarily in private rice fields in farming communities. They were found largely in fresh water marshes, and in some of California's NWR-protected marshes.

I hope many of the readers of this book will make a trip to a great area of our nation to hunt marsh hens, and enjoy doing it in the traditional manner of poling the marsh with a guide, and sit on that front gunner's chair and relieve the marsh and the grand sport of hunting rail that makes all sportsmen a little better wing shot in the pursuit of this noble marsh bird.

Everyone was most kind all across America, even those Audubon researchers and the few anti-hunter birders that I met in California and on the Texas Gulf coast during the winter and spring, who gave me a piece of their mind. However, both they and I were appreciative of enlightened discussions, especially in reference to the endangered California King rail and the environmental issues impacting that particular species.

Scholars will note that as I have pursued Sora and Clapper rails for over forty years, and I have quite different experiences, and observations from a hunter, guide and researcher from scientific studies. However, they as a whole were most interested that I had studied every scientific paper ever written on all the sub-species of rail birds, and that my book will be a future and important source reference on the five rail birds found in North America. As my assignments during peacetime have allowed me the ability to travel and hunt rail birds across the American flyways, my studies and journal notes within this book are quite important in the sportsman's education of these species.

I hope that foundations such as DU and DELTA will encourage more study, and that there can be a more thorough banding data sample in the future, beginning in the spring from each of the flyways across Canada of the major huntable rail bird species: Clapper, Sora, Virginia and King . At the least, there should be a three-year limited bird band study of all four huntable species in the Canadian James Bay Marshes, via traps and selective yet limited banding, especially in the Atlantic Flyway states.

I have attempted to put together the most scholarly hunting book ever written on the Rallidae species, as well as the history of the areas, towns, and communities where rail hunting has left an indelible and positive mark upon all the people, places, rail guides, families and friends through the gunning of this unique species.

Parental Care of the young brood: Both parents attend the chicks in the early stages of development of the Species. Adams and Quay (1958) reflect in their North Carolina study, that "…while one parent brooded newly hatched chicks and incubated any remaining eggs, the other parent would lead the first hatched chicks a short way from the protection of the nest." I have seen a great many times where one rail bird parent attempt to lead me off in an opposite direction- by appearing to have a broken wing (dragging it) in a obvious attempt to draw me away from the brood, which I noticed was quickly swimming away with the other parent. I do see a great deal of nesting clappers in the brackish marshes off behind the Sea Islands off North Carolina while poling my skiff and fly fishing during warm flood tide days that occur in late March or early April.

Adams and Quay (1957) in their King and Clapper rail bird studies stated that they would even observe the parental-care period into the sixth week after hatching, when chicks happened to be caught in one of their research traps, the parents of King or Clapper rail birds would invariantly be just five or ten feet away hiding, and watching over their young. The newly hatched rail bird chick is covered with a coal black down and that down is present for most of the first month, however it shows some white especially around its underpants areas of its body as those feathers begin to develop, and quills appear in most little rail birds by the sixty day period. In the Juvenile stages, *R.E. Steward* notes in his 1965 study that, "…by August, the larger young rail birds can be distinguished from the adults via the olive-green iris instead of the orange, or orange-brown iris; and the bills on the Juvenile are more pinkish-slate gray.

RESEARCH & ANALYSIS OF THE RAIL BIRD SPECIES–MIGRATORY LESSONS LEARNED

Research and analysis has shown the educated wildfowler that beginning with the 1952–1953 hunting season, the U.S. Fish and Wildlife Service (FWS) has compiled data with regard to annual surveys of Federal Duck Stamp purchasers, in order to estimate waterfowl hunter activity and migratory wildfowl and waterfowl harvest data in the United States. The FWS survey was conducted annually through the 2001-02 hunting season, after which it was replaced by a new migratory game bird harvest survey system.

In 1992, the FWS and the state Fish and Wildlife Agencies established the Migratory Bird Harvest Information Program (HIP), which became fully Operational nationwide in 1999.

I have personally recommended in my conversations and written comments that the US FWS Migratory Bird Department institute a "limited banding program" to focus first and primarily on the Atlantic Flyway for all species of rail birds (Clapper, Virginia, King and Sora) in the future. Although numbering in the millions along the Atlantic Flyway's river and tidal deltas, they are primarily gunned along the salt marshes of the Atlantic Flyway, especially during the limited number of flood tide days.

However, during the other days of the maximum allowable seventy-day season for rail bird hunting, these species are not hunted much at all, due primarily to the rigors of poling a boat in the rail bird's native habitat: the salt marsh Spartina grass flats, or the inshore fresh water marshes, and rice fields all along the eastern seaboard inshore waters or rivers, or those impoundments that have built for waterfowl hunting for private waterfowl hunting throughout the Flyways of North America.

Rail birds are hunted in far less numbers throughout the freshwater marshes, impoundments and delta marshes along the lakes and rivers of the Mississippi Flyway, and the impoundments and marshes of the freshwater lakes along the Central Flyway. A cooperative state-federal program was developed and designed in order to provide each year an appropriate sample-frame for FWS national surveys of licensed migratory bird hunters. This includes those who hunt species for which adequate harvest information was lacking.

HIP requires licensed migratory bird hunters to identify themselves as such annually, to the state licensing authority, and provide the state their name, address, and date of birth, and carry evidence of their compliance whenever they hunt migratory birds in that state. States are required to collect this information from each licensed migratory bird hunter, provide migratory bird hunters with proof of compliance, and ask each hunter a series of screening questions about their hunting success the previous year. All states must provide all of the HIP survey information to the FWS within 30 days of its collection. The Fish and Wildlife Service is responsible for using this data provided by the states in order to conduct a national hunter activity, and harvest surveys, each year for each of these "migratory (webless) game bird(s)," as they are a unique migratory webless species and subspecies of migratory marsh bird. Yet some subspecies, such as the California King Rail (CKR) living in the Pacific Flyway, have been on the endangered species list in the State of California since 1971, and all rail bird species are closed throughout that state. That has not always been the case, as the Clapper and Sora are still migratory in the Great Bear State, even with the environmental problems of the Sacramento Delta Region upon the CKR. The more adaptable Clapper survives and grows in numbers. I strongly urge that more banding be done on all the rail bird species in the Pacific region over a three-year period, with a team of California wildfowl biologists seeking a better understanding of the rail bird species in this particular flyway.

Although the Clapper rail (*Rallus longirostris*) has been a game bird of great importance throughout the middle and south Atlantic and Gulf Coast regions since the days of Audubon, the Atlantic King (*Rallus elegans*) rail is the largest of the species, and is quite healthy in population, as is the Sora (Carolina porosia). These two rail bird species prefer early in their migratory periods to eat wild rice whenever it's available, and enjoy primarily the diverse habitats of fresh water, or very low salinity and brackish marshes. The *primary food sources* for the Clapper rail are in order of importance: fiddler crabs, marsh grasshoppers, and the periwinkle/spartina snails. The Sora thrives on Wild Rice as their primary food source and inveribrates as secondary food sources. Rail birds are most loyal parents to its young chicks, which are born jet black, and do their best to protect their clutch, and hatchlings in the marsh.

The Clapper rail/Marsh hen is the most dominant and most gunned species of marsh bird; found throughout the Central and Atlantic Flyway and the Gulf marshes. However, because of their migratory nature and habitat, hunting them can be most difficult and quite labor intensive due to the heavy amount of poling that must be done during flood tide periods in massive sized marshes. In 1926, Bent wrote his first scientific studies of this species, but little had been scientifically written on this species between Bent's research and John J. Audubon's 1809, 1811, and 1843 journal entries of his rail bird hunting expeditions, and observations of this species. Witmer Stone (1932) had some excellent natural history research done on Clapper rails at Cape May, New Jersey; as did the Cobb Island, Virginia, studies of nesting and breeding of Clapper rails in 1933, and again in 1938 when Petingill expounded upon lessons learned and his own unique observations in light of Witmer Stone's 1937 research compiled on breeding pairs, nesting trends, food sources, and observations of the Clapper rail in tidal salt marshes and migration of the species along the Atlantic Flyway.

Although four huntable species are indeed found throughout the flyways of North America, three species are seen more frequently by rail bird hunters along the coastal salt marshes. In reviewing my personal journals and observations over forty years of hunting rail birds in the Atlantic Flyway, I see a distinct, yet very limited joint migration occurring within the Sora, Virginia, and Clapper rail bird communities. Therefore, I also find that all species will inhabit a general, yet defined marsh area, especially during a very limited time period following a great storm. Normally the migratory world of the rail bird I have seen the sora migrate succinctly southward to the southeastern New Jersey wild rice meadows, after that they move more with other species when storm fronts, cold fronts push down with such furiosity that migratory birds push out together as a group.

I do find a surprising number of Clapper and Sora more often together in North Carolina coastal inshore brackish water marshes. However, they are often congregated in certain locations, and in succinct marsh complexes within delta regions where there is less salinity, due to the massive fresh water flowing into the regions. Yet along the South Carolina coastal inshore waters, with the exception of the confluence of the ACE Basin river system in the southeastern state, and where the North and South Santee rivers meet the Atlantic Ocean south of Georgetown, South Carolina, I have found very few numbers of Sora, even those close to freshwater rice impoundments.

Perhaps this is more due to the Sora's preference for rice, and the fact that there are fewer numbers of working rice fields remaining along the South Carolina coastal inshore due to the high cost of this particular crop. The older rice fields that once adjourned the freshwater rivers have dwindled due to the continued dredging necessary for commercial barge traffic, naval ships, and submarines. This has created heaver flood tides, pushing more salinity into the fresh water mix, and salt marshes are taking over the old wild rice that used to dominate the South Carolina river system in the low country.

The Sora and King rails rarely if ever migrate together, and there is zero research to reflect otherwise. Yet there is a significant amount of inter-migration between the King and the

Clapper, although the Atlantic Clapper rail appears to be interbreeding more often with the Clapper, as they interact more throughout the migration periods of the fall and spring. Kings, which have an affinity for fresh water marshes, do NOT follow the migrations of the earlier Sora rail bird, nor are there hunting journal accounts that offer more historical insight to their movements regarding early migrations along the traditional fresh water rice meadows.

King rails tend to migrate southward with their larger cousins, the Clapper, yet along that migratory path they move inland and congregate primarily in the fresh water marshes further westward during full moon migrations . The stronger and more numerous Clapper rail, along with the diminutive little Sora, are the dominant and larger species of rail bird in terms of numbers, and can be found throughout the tidal saline and brackish fresh water marshes along the Eastern Seaboard and the Atlantic and Mississippi Flyways.

The Central and Pacific Flyways' populations of Sora and Clapper have not been studied as much as the Pacific King (California King) rail bird, hereafter referred to as CKR. However, there are some limited ornithological and biological studies, as noted in my bibliography. The CKR has been listed as endangered throughout the Pacific Flyway, and that region's rail seasons have been closed or severely limited—just as rail bird hunting in the state of California been banned—due to DNR wildfowl biologists studies on the CKR. This flyway has not done a proper or thorough rail bird study since the very limited band study in 1971, as funding for band research has not been a priority to those in senior leadership in the DNR, which I certainly hope will change with more letters to the department. I hope to see future planning committees get in line with future financial planning ideals.

There are *zero* scientific studies by the U.S. DFG Wildfowl/Waterfowl division's Migratory Bird Band department of the rail bird, except for two brief bird band studies of limited scope in 1965 and 1971. I have noted a lack of scientific studies in the banding program related to rail bird hunting, yet more money is spent on telemetry studies, which have a tiny success rate due to its weight and size in reflection of this species. Really, all those studies are quite limited in scope, and are not conducive to the major effort a three-year bird banding study could bring to better graphing more in-depth studies along all the North American Flyways, and westward across the nation to the lakes and marshes and impoundments where you can find the little Sora rail and a limited number of Clapper, King, and Virginia rails in freshwater marshes and impoundments, and especially in the managed rice fields during September and October as the rice matures.

More Sora rails can be found along the Atlantic Flyway throughout their migration southward along that most ancient of rivers: the Mississippi. Ol' Miss has seen the sky blanketed with migrations throughout the centuries, and the Sora can be found in the marshes of private impoundments and marshy lakes as that species migrates southward ahead of the cold fronts of October and November that push down the Mississippi and Central Flyways. Most modern-day wildfowlers do not realize that the rails are down in such numbers if they do not keep up with the marsh bird. In fact, most hunters in the Mississippi Flyway are more interested in their managed wetlands and rice fields being developed more for mallard ducks and other waterfowl species, than the red-headed stepchild of the wildfowl community that are the rail birds of today. Perhaps their disposition has allowed them to grow in such numbers not seen by most wildfowlers of that flyway.

RAIL BIRD INFORMATION FOR SETTING LIMITS AND DATES BY STATE AND MIGRATORY WILDFOWL COMMISSIONS

Outside Dates: States included herein may select seasons between September 1 and the last Sunday in January (January 29) for Clapper, King, Sora, and Virginia rails.

Hunting Seasons: Seasons may not exceed 70 days, and may be split into 2 segments.

Daily Bag Limits: **Clapper** and **King** Rails—In Rhode Island, Connecticut, New Jersey, Delaware, and Maryland, 15, singly or in the aggregate of the 2 species.

In Texas, Louisiana, Mississippi, Alabama, Georgia, Florida, South Carolina, North Carolina, and Virginia, 15, singly or in the aggregate of the two species.

Sora and **Virginia Rails**—In the Atlantic, Mississippi, and Central Flyways and the Pacific Flyway portions of Colorado, Montana, New Mexico, and Wyoming: 25 daily and 25 in possession, singly or in the aggregate of the two species.

The season is CLOSED in the remainder of the Pacific Flyway, as the **California King rail** is a protected and endangered species!

HIP Statistical data and analysis (snap shot) of rail bird hunters throughout the USA, and looking at hunters that hunted rail birds, and numbers listed in these studies as rail birds harvested as a group: during of specific seasons of: (1999-2000), (2001-2002), and (2011 and 2012).

Look at the numbers of rail birds killed, and number of rail bird hunters across the country, from figures compiled from this HIP Study Data, which was provided to me by the U.S. Department of Fish and Wildlife's Migratory Bird Division over six rail bird seasons: the 1999 to 2012 migratory rail bird season Hunter Information Program reports. The differences between 1999 and 2000 are significant:

- 1999: 11,900 hunters listed; 31,600 rail birds harvested (+41%)
- 2000: 6,900 hunters listed; 15,300 rail birds harvested (+56%)

According to the National Wildfowl Migratory Species Survey and my personal research reports, the following hunting statistical data was reported:

- 2001: 6,000 hunters harvested 41,200 rail birds (+75%)
- 2002: 23,800 rail birds harvested (+/- 48%)
- 2009: 7,800 hunters harvested 36,100 rail birds (+/-62%)
- 2010: 17,000 hunters harvested 27,100 rail birds (+/-57%)
- 2011: 16,500 hunters harvested 26,500 rail birds
- 2012: 17,250 hunters harvested 31,350 rail birds

Under the above reporting data, each separate subspecies of Rallidae were simply classified (Rail), and there is no accurate data of the subspecies: Clapper, Sora, Virginia, or King Rail birds.

*I would ask all my readers to please take the time and effort to write a personal letter to the US FWS (Migratory Bird Division) to request a complete subspecies listing in future HIP Surveys, including what state and counties were hunted in, which would be more informative and allow the researcher to better gather specific scientific data on all the rail birds in order to follow each subspecies hunted, and so the regions where stronger numbers of birds and hunters are found can be better determined.

In your letter to the USFWD Migratory Bird Banding Department, please mention your support for more rail bird banding to be included in that department's next budget, and that a "three-year scientific study of their migratory nature" would be vastly important to future generations of rail bird wildfowlers, who happen to also provide donations and finances each and every year to DU and Delta Wildfowl research programs, as well as the USDFG Migratory Bird Stamp Program, which need to be aligned to "all migratory web and webless birds," and especially all huntable migratory species. These additional migratory financial increases should demand more bird banding and research studies on all our huntable rail bird species. This is something that should be an increased priority in the near future, to ensure a deeper scientific study of each of the four huntable rail bird species across North America. After all, they are migratory game birds, and deserve more attention and research.

Through the years, I have seen a great many waterfowl migration patterns change—due, I believe, to a combination of global warming, drought conditions, changes in row crop rotation along the Atlantic coastal seaboard, and wildlife refuges not planting corn and flooding it along the major flyways across our great nation. However, our rail bird populations along the Atlantic Flyway have continued to grow through the years, with the exception of the state of California and their endangered California King Rail. Dredging allows saltwater intrusion into the freshwater rivers, and over time destroys wild rice meadows. Runoff from industrial plants and golf courses, along with farming practices near estuary wilderness regions, sometimes allow chemical waste into the ecosystem. This negatively impacts the marshes, killing important grasses and wildlife, and adding to the destruction of the natural resources of that environment.

Being sportsmen and hunters, we all must realize that the Atlantic Flyway's King rail has been interbreeding with the Clapper rail and morphing into some mighty large Clapper/King hybrid rail birds over the years. The same thing happens to mallards and black ducks during migration and cohabitation. Rail birds sleeping together! What is causing this to happen within those two Atlantic Flyway species is currently chalked up to "interbreeding of these two sub-species of rail birds," and no federal funding is currently available to study this situation. However, there is a great deal of funding in California and the federal government in order to try to save the Pacific Flyway's King Rail.

Like other Pacific Flyway water fowl, Pacific rail birds do not cross over from Atlantic to Pacific flyways. Therefore, it's safe to assume that the Pacific King rail bird needs more creative means to try to revive that particular species, or wildlife biologists need to resort to trapping some Atlantic Flyway King Rails, so they can introduce that subspecies to their Pacific cousins and hope that the stronger Atlantic Flyway King rail can develop and assist in reestablishing the breeding habits of their West Coast cousin.

Of course, this type of thinking would take quite a bit of study and effort and a great deal of grant money, and that may not be feasible to the CA-DNR, or to those California wildfowler researchers and various water bird societies currently trying to get the California King Rail bird off the endangered species list, and have a healthy population growth once again throughout the freshwater marshes of the California Delta region.

Ken Sheen Virginia Rail carving, 1977

MERCURY CONTAMINTION STUDY ON GEORGIA RAILS

I always am always learning and studying, and trying to better understand why more research has not been infused into the DNR Bird Banding Division for longer scientific studies of rail bird species. Banding was done two major times with rail birds, in 1965 and 1971, according to the BBD of the NDR. This in itself needs to be addressed by more senior administrative people, in order to reestablish a consistent rail bird banding program, especially focused on the Sora, the Clapper, the Virginia, and the Atlantic King rails. Particularly on the west coast of the U.S., in the Pacific Flyway, there needs to be more banding done on the endangered California King Rail.

What concerns me even greater is the terrible lack of rail bird banding data being done. This needs to be addressed and I suggest that more banding is done in the future, at least in each flyway in North America, by wildlife researchers in a joint effort from the U.S. and Canada.

I came across what is almost a forgotten study by Mr. Ron R. Odom for the Georgia Department of Natural Resources. It is a very interesting statistical analysis of mercury contamination in Georgia rail birds, during which rail birds and salt marsh aquatic food species samples were taken and tested for mercury contamination in a number of different Brunswick and Turtle River Estuary salt marsh areas during these two specific time periods: October 1971 and September 1973. This unique study and its findings were published under the title: Mercury Contamination Study in Georgia Rail Birds by Ron R. Odom, GA-DNR-Game and Fish Division. The Turtle River-Brunswick River Area, which is upstream from Brunswick, Georgia; and the Savannah River, running from Augusta to Savannah, had been identified in the years of 1970 and 1971 as being very heavily contaminated with mercury, discharged for many years by the chlorine-alkali plants which manufactured chlorine and caustic soda through the electrolysis of brine and used mercury as an electrode.

In 1970, Allied and Olin chemical plants reported discharges of three and ten pounds per day, respectively into the adjacent waters. Discharges in both plants had quickly been reduced to less than .025 pounds per day (Georgia Water Quality Control Board 1971 Report on Mercury Contamination by A & O). In the Brunswick Estuary, mercury contamination generally was found to be greater than the .050 ppm limit, as set by the U.S. Food and Drug Administration (USFDA), in the blue crab, speckled trout, and flounder. Subsequently, the Georgia State Game and Fish Division banned all fishing and crabbing in the Brunswick Estuary, and in the Savannah River from Augusta to Savannah.

Later, as concentrations of mercury in aquatic samples decreased, the ban on fishing and crabbing was eventually lifted. In 1973, the State Department of Natural Resources and the EPA issued a warning to hunters not to eat Clapper rails taken <u>upstream</u> from the HWY 17 Bridge in the Brunswick Estuary, due to the discovery of very high mercury residues in Clapper rail bird sampling. In accordance with USDA and EPA guidelines, scientific sampling was done from 1970-1971. However, it was restricted to fish, crabs, shrimp, and shellfish, with no attempt to monitor levels in marsh birds or mammals within the contaminated areas, even though birds and mammals both were present in very large numbers, and were an integral part of the salt marsh ecosystem.

Specimens were collected in nine different locations, and "breast tissue samples" were properly coded and secured for shipment, in order to do a proper scientific study and analysis of exactly what was the parts per million (ppm) of mercury contamination found in the various species within the scientific sampling, including rail birds, blue and fiddler crabs, and the Spartina snails (periwinkle) that grow or attach to Spartina grass stalks. These snails are food species for sporting fish and other crab species, and in their juvenile stages of development they may be eaten by Clapper rails foraging in the salt marshes. Core samples taken in 1971 from the Brunswick Estuary revealed the presence of mercury in sediments to a minimum depth of twelve inches. Samples at depths greater than these were not taken (Zeller and Finger 1971).

The salt marsh in the Brunswick Estuary supports an extremely large population of Clapper rails, which are hunted by a growing number of sportsmen each fall. Large numbers of Sora rails also use these same marshes during periods of migration, through seldom are the Sora rail birds hunted.

Possible contamination, particularly of the potentially important Clapper rail and its food chain, was suspected. Therefore, collections of rails birds and rail food items were initiated at various locations along the Georgia Coast inshore waters. Of primary concern among researchers and the scientific community was the levels of mercury present in the eatable portion of the marsh hen (breast meat), which might be ingested by wildfowl hunters. Richard Gingrich of the EPA originally recognized the potential mercury problem in rail birds, and requested and initiated the 1971 collections.

Heavy stand of wild rice obscures this rail boat on the Maurice River, N.J.

CHAPTER SEVEN
BOATS, MOTORS, & OTHER HUNTING GEAR

When the tide starts dropping, we need to get our light, shallow water boats out of the salt marsh and into deeper water to head back to the landing. You need to know your tides, and the high and low meadows and marshes, as well as keep up with the migration too. Each season, I see some of those expensive flats boats that some guides are using today, which may draft as much as 12 inches depending on their design and weight capabilities when fully loaded. Large technical skiffs such as the Hewes Craft, Hells Bay, and Action Craft will draft too much, in my personal opinion, and are just too heavy a boat to be used along the southeast coastal salt marshes for rail bird hunting, except for limited time during the highest of flood tides. However, there are a handful of lighter technical skiffs, such as the Beavertail, Mitzi, and Ranger Ghost technical skiffs, which will draft closer to 6 inches. These can be used in some of the Carolina and Georgia salt marsh Spartina grass flats, where 6.5 to 9.5 foot high tides occur in September, October, and November.

Sixteen-foot, 30-year-old Railbird hunting Skiff with fifteen-foot handcrafted push poles–for wild rice meadows in NE USA

Sonny returning home from a rail bird hunt

Canoe with outboard–tows rail bird skiffs to NJ rice meadows–JP Hand Photo 2009

 Of course, those large flats boats are really made for crossing large bodies of water, and for technical poling once you've arrived on a particular flat. However, I would like to point out that there are large Jon boats out there on the market that draft < 4 inches, and a very few that will draft less than 3 inches with three people. My 19' x 69" D3 Marsh Master Skiff was specially made for poling in skinny water, and is a dream to pole in any salt marsh from Maryland south through the Carolinas, Georgia and Florida.

There are just not enough high tides available along the Gulf coasts to float any heavy technical skiffs (modern flats boats) in western Florida, Alabama, Louisiana, or Texas. Most of 'em are just too heavy and draft too much to get in and out of Spartina grass flats with any confidence, but you could push up and along some creeks and pound the grass points with your push pole.

No matter what state I'm hunting rail birds in, there are some who love the hunt and are always reluctant to leave. We may have been out during a super tide during September or October, or some exceptionally high tides in the new moon or full moon periods of November and December along the South Atlantic states. Perhaps you were not watching the water table drop, or perhaps the winds that were pushing the water and increasing the lunar tidal heights were no longer blowing as strong, or had switched directions—and you suddenly realize that you've got to get out of there quickly.

Sora Rail Birds + VA rail- 28ga SxS (Darryl Bogard photo)

If you don't have a light skiff, perhaps you need to get a light Jon boat, or a special wooden handmade rail boat like those you see in this book, or you might very well find yourself stuck out in the marsh, and you may have to wait seven or eight hours for the tides to return in order to get your heavier boat or skiff out of that flat. So learn to read the tides and the winds, and your distance from a deep exit point, anytime you are poling across a rail bird flat or wild rice meadow—no matter what type of rail bird hunting boat you're using.

Be smart, be safe, and have a boating plan to cover a particular distance poling. Set your watch alarm with enough time to get out of a flooded flat with your rig, and follow your hunt safety plan. If the winds are blowing and pushing water, stacking it up higher in a particular flat that you happen to be hunting, then realize you may have a little more time. If you are lucky, it could extend the tidal height as much as +/- 30 minutes, or an extra hour more than your printed tide chart. You've just got to learn how to judge these conditions and tides over time, and hopefully not get stranded because you waited too long to chase rail birds around a particular flooded flat that is suddenly falling off quicker than expected.

Be observant of the tide levels, and agree with your boat mates over when you need to get off the water—unless you have a guide who know the area, and knows exactly how much time you have to stay in a flat or rice meadow and pursue rail birds before the tide drops precipitously. I have found that a handheld GPS is invaluable in finding the closest deep creek to get off the flat or marsh as quickly as possible. It is an essential item to have on board my boat.

Mrs. Sara had a good hunt day

Sora rail bird hunting in the blown down wild rice meadows of Merrymeeting Bay, Maine.

CHAPTER EIGHT
RAIL HUNTING THE NORTHEASTERN STATES

Merrymeeting Bay's marshes have been historical for wildfowl hunting throughout history—and they are grand marshes, where rail birds can be found in September and early October. However, there is very little rail bird hunting happening there today. Too many other hunting opportunities draw the attention of the modern-day hunter, who spends time pursuing larger game, upland bird hunting, and waterfowling. There are five major rail bird rivers that flow into Merrymeeting Bay.

The five rivers in total that make up this vast bay have significant acreage of wild rice meadows. These rivers are the Kennebec, Cathance, Abbagadassett, Eastern, and the Androscoggin. The "Bay," as it's referred to by the locals, is very large—approximately twenty miles long by perhaps ten miles wide. Wild rice meadows abound, with tall stands of rice that have continued to grow and regroup over the years, ever since it was first planted by Native Americans.

Arrowheads have been found along the mud flats, where the rice meadows grow up to eight feet high. Old timers still hunt in traditional Merrymeeting Bay sculling boats. Sixteen feet in length, with very pointy bows for getting through the wild rice, these boats are towed into the hunt area and then pushed by a wooden push pole, with the gunner standing or sitting in the bow of the wooden skiffs.

Currently the Maine rail bird season starts September 1st and ends in early November, and there is no Sunday hunting in Maine. However, there is a growing wealthy population building grander and grander homes along the banks of that most majestic of Maine rivers, and there has been an increase in environmentalists and other individuals migrating to Maine, who seem to not care very much for hunting of any kind.

Today, there is very little rail bird hunting being done along the banks of that once great and most majestic of Maine rivers that historically had some of the greatest numbers of migratory Sora rail birds and waterfowl passing through these fresh waters to chow down on the wild rice, until the first bit of cold weather starts blowing its chilly breath from way up north in Canada. Maine rail bird season should probably open much earlier, in reality, around the first flood tide in August. By the first flood tide of October, most of the migratory rail birds in Maine's wild rice meadows have already moved on, ever southward.

I therefore make this recommendation to Maine's migratory game bird committee, and I certainly hope that more wildfowlers will get the opportunity to see just how beautiful these Maine wild rice meadows are all around Merrymeeting Bay, and of course those five major rivers that flow into the Bay.

Over the years, there has been some grand rail bird hunting along those rice meadows—mostly Sora rail, but there is also a small migration of Virginia rail birds that arrive with the flood tides in September. Like the Sora, they quickly move southward when the cold fronts of October come roaring down the coast from Canada and the Maritime Providences.

Rail hunting all around the Delaware Bay and the beautiful rice meadows that lie along the banks of the Maurice River has been discussed and done by hundreds of thousands of sportsmen since the early 1850s. Sora rail was, of course, the predominant species, with a bag limit of twenty-five rail birds per person effective in the 1933 season. Wealthy sportsmen used to take a room for the night of their hunt, or prior to it, at the famous Mauricetown Hotel in Mauricetown, New Jersey, where the boats and pushers were furnished for anywhere from $20 to $75 per hunt tide.

Navy Pilot Ray Moses zeros in on an outgoing King rail (Joe Guide)

Today, a guided rail bird hunt with a professional guide will cost you close to $500 for a flood tide period of poling through the rice meadows of the Maurice River. If you are very lucky and don't miss too many rail birds, and if ol' General Average and Lady Luck is with you, my friend, you might get your limit of 25 Sora rails birds before the end of your second box of shells! Furthermore, if the winds are pushing the flood tide higher than prescribed, and the Sora's are flying mighty fast, you might need one more box of shells than you think. So pack your gear for your next rail bird hunting trip carefully.

The Sora are still as numerous today on the Walking and the Maurice Rivers of southern New Jersey as they were prior to the Great War, and some days I wonder if perhaps even more birds might migrate through this regional area today than prior to 1939. Some of my readers might find that statement rather hard to fathom, but it's certainly true. However, the locals aren't talking. They all know a good thing, and don't really desire a massive number of gunners to come flooding into that part of southern New Jersey prior to the first flood tide in September.

Do you realize that wildfowling Presidents such as Teddy Roosevelt, well before he became Alderman in New York City, and other famous sportsmen throughout the years came to hunt rail in Mauricetown, New Jersey? No matter where you go to gun rail, there is one thing that never changes, which is that it still takes a lot of hard work poling your shallow water skiff in order to get to those birds to jump out of the marsh during a flood tide. Traditionally it's only done during the highest of tides, and if you desire to go, you've got to book a trip as early as possible!

Of course, this is true for all the major rail bird gunning states in the Atlantic Flyway. The same could be said along the freshwater marsh impoundments off the Mississippi Flyway, as well as the great Clapper rail bird marshes all along the Atlantic coastal seaboard—from Connecticut River's dwindling rice meadows, to the South Jersey rivers, and ever southward as the rail bird flies along the Atlantic Flyway. All the way down, to those salt marshes behind Amelia Island, Florida, or about as far south as they go to the Indian River Marshes outside of Titusville, Florida.

SOME FAMOUS RAIL BIRD HUNTERS

There were a great number of captains of industry who hunted these same historic marshes off the Connecticut River rice meadows, or further south off Delaware Bay and New Jersey. Some of these famous gunners traveled south along the Atlantic Seaboard and enjoyed gunning for rail birds back in the days of their youth. Carnegie, Fisk, J.J. Astor, and the Rockefeller boys—all were keen rail gunners. There was President Abraham Lincoln's former Secretary of State Hamilton Fish, who later would take his young grandson Hamilton Fish Jr. rail bird hunting with him. This was years prior to young Ham's date with destiny in the jungles of Las Gusimas, Cuba, with the 1st U.S. Cavalry while serving with the "Rough Riders."

History notes that a number of U.S. Presidents gunned those same rice marshes in southern New Jersey, including such dignitaries as Benjamin Harrison, Grover Cleveland, Theodore "Teddy" Roosevelt, and as the log books will note, even his young cousin Franklin Delano Roosevelt, while he was still a young fellow (and at the time Deputy Secretary of the Navy, prior to WWI under Josephus Daniels).

Were you readers aware, that two Generals of the Army, Douglas A. McArthur and John J. Pershing, were keen rail gunners? Yes sir, McArthur's father and Pershing shot rail birds in eastern Virginia, and young Doug did, too. Ask the historian at the McArthur Museum in Norfolk, VA to please show you a photo of Douglas' shotgun collection. History notes that General Pershing was the better shot (see the West Point Skeet Club Records of his skeet shoot with McArthur when he was Commandant). "Blackjack" Pershing shot a Fox 20ga SxS quail gun, and occasionally a custom made Parker 20 SxS with 28-inch barrels. Douglas McArthur shot a Parker 20ga SxS, which was also his father's favorite shotgun.

Were you aware that those two famous Generals (father and son) were each awarded the Medal of Honor? Lt Gen Arthur MacArthur was awarded his MOH for capturing a battle flag during a battle in the great Civil War, and Douglas for his service and leadership during the early days of WWII in the Philippines.

Douglas was recommended in dispatches two earlier times for high decorations, one was for his work in a secret scouting expedition deep behind enemy lines, this occurred following the "Tampico Affair" of April 9, 1914 in Tampico, Tamaulipas. This little known armed conflict occurred after armed US Sailors were arrested for entering a fuel loading station to purchase fuel in that port town.

This incident escalated due that the Naval Commander demanded a formal apology, which did not occur, primarily due to poor Mexican diplomatic relations, and this incident- erupted into armed conflict in the port town of Veracruz. Mexican National Troops from their Naval and Armed Forces along with US Naval and ground forces, including a detachment of US Marine Fleet Marine Forces that encompassed the US Naval Expeditionary Forces (NEF) into the back country of Veracruz, Mexico. At the time, young Doug MacArthur was just a young 1st Lt. For all you arm chair historians, please note that this incident was President Woodrow Wilson's- second real test of foreign policy and of the Presidential War Powers Clause in the Constitution, in his decision to occupy the port of Veracruz. If the armed attack upon US Forces was not enough, it was also due to his receiving an intercepted cable, that the Germany had supply ships delivering weapons for Victoriano Hureta aboard the German-Flagged Steamer SS YPIRANGA. This particular incident reminded President Kennedy early in his Presidency, and therefore assisted him to make up his mind, in regard to stopping the Russian supply ships carrying missiles that were enroute to Cuba at sea by the use of a Naval blockade.

MacArthur ended up marring Pershing's old girlfriend after WWI, an attractive socialite from Philadelphia, Pennsylvania. You may not be aware that Doug was recommended for a MOH as a Colonel in WWI, for volunteering to lead a scouting party at night into no man's land. Douglas eventually became the youngest Brigadier General to come out of the Great War from the AEF. However, that paperwork was eventually downgraded to a Silver Star by….General Pershing! Imagine that.

Lt General Julian Smith, USMC, commanded the 2d MARDIV (FMF) during the Bloody Battle of Tarawa. He was born and bred in Elkhorn, Maryland, and liked to call himself an "old rail hunter from Chesapeake Bay" who loved hunting both the nearby Assateague's and eastern Virginia's Chincoteague's grand ol' rail bird marshes. General Julian (that was what his marines called him) when he was young officer, had once commanded the Marine Corps Rifle Team, and was a grand shot with his Winchester 20ga SxS shotgun. He also shot rail birds off the lower Cape Fear River delta marshes behind Bald Head Island, as a guest of the James L. Sprunt family of Wilmington, North Carolina, before and after WWII.

The Sprunts were a family of wealthy cotton importers and exporters to England, prior to and following the War of Northern Aggression, and they were one of the richest families along the North Carolina coast for a great many years. General Smith was a familiar guest down around Georgetown and Charleston, South Carolina, too. Bernard W. Baruch, the great Wall Street tycoon and financial confidant to Coolidge, Hoover, and FDR during their presidencies, owned a massive wildfowl hunting lodge off Winyah Bay's North Point Sea Islands, outside of Georgetown, South Carolina, and invited hundreds of famous guests and politicians over the years on wildfowl hunting trips from 1911 to 1947. That property is now managed by the Belle W. Baruch Foundation and some family relations, lawyers and such up in NYC. Baruch also enjoyed his friend Archibald Rutledge's favorite rail bird hunting marshes of McCleanville, South Carolina. These marshes are now part of the Cape Romain National Wildlife Refuge.

Lt General Chesty Puller, USMC, was awarded five Navy Crosses for gallantry in combat during the "Banana Wars" in Nicaragua, WWII, and Korea. Chesty got introduced to rail bird hunting with General Julian Smith after WWII, when Puller was assigned to Camp Lejeune, North Carolina. Puller, in his personal journals, seemed to prefer quail to rail bird hunting, as he said, "Rail bird hunting was mighty hard work for old men, but not young Marines."

Andy Griffith hunted rail birds, although he always got a local guide and hunted the marshes off the lower Cape Fear, and up north in Mauricetown, New Jersey when he was living in NYC. Many famous gentlemen in sports gunned for rail birds, such as baseball great George "Babe" Ruth, Ted Williams of the Boston Red Sox, and Jim "Catfish" Hunter, who grew up along the northeastern coast of eastern North Carolina.

Three rail-hunting former Presidents had local rail hunting guides, pole their handmade wooden poles and homemade light weight wooden skiffs during flood tides along the wild rice meadows off the Patuxent and the Maurice River, during those few special days when the full and new moon flood tides rolled around each September and October back in their day. Walter and Rich Camp were just "young'uns" when they first started guiding sportsmen through the marshes for rail hunting. "Now, other Camp family members such as cousins and nephews take out the push pole and old wooden rail skiffs there to this day, said Darrel Bogue", a local gunsmith and a close friend of Walter Camp who lives nearby. They guided most every September and October during flood tide days, and loved every adventure and memory! There are still some Camps living around Dorchester and Port Elizabeth today, and you can be sure that they all are watermen and rail bird hunters through and through.

In the last twenty-five years of the 19th century, well over a hundred thousand Sora rails were gunned over the rice fields along the Maurice River. I have seen a hunting journal from the West Jersey Game Protection Society describing one super high tide day in October, 1888, when 197 gunners shot their limit of rail in less than one hour of poling.

A great secret kept is something that's hard to grasp for too long. Therefore, I will tell you readers that Sora are still as abundant in great numbers today on the Maurice and Walking Rivers during the months of September and October, as they were in the early 20th century—but you need to get after them during a flood tide! These days, it's quite possible that three gunners, being poled across a couple of miles of wild rice meadows by three good guides, can kill their limit of twenty-five Sora rail in under an hour if there is a strong Northeaster pushing a lunar tide higher than normal. That is an extremely liberal 75 Sora rail bird legal limit for those three friends out rail bird hunting on a super flood tide day. However you should understand, that those kinds of hunting days, don't happen that often, but just when certain conditions (winds and tide) all come together to create a super high tide during rail bird hunting season.

However, you must remember that you've got to go hunting only on the highest of high tides, and preferably with a good local guide, as the highest normal September and October tides might only last for 90 minutes or so. If you are lucky to go when a northeastern wind is blowing, then you might get to stay out as long as 120 minutes with this super high tide conditions, due to the winds from up north pushing the water levels much higher than normal and extending the tidal period.

There are only four to six super high tides each season in the fall months of September and October in the northeastern coastal states, when the tides are at their highest levels during sunlight hours. I think you will agree that twenty-five Sora rail are a most generous bag limit per person, even in our present day and time, and that's also the limit in the majority of our rail bird hunting states of Connecticut, Delaware, Maryland, Virginia, North Carolina, South Carolina, Georgia, and Florida. However, there will probably only be a couple of skiffs poling a particular section of rice meadow for rail on any given flood tide day. So, as you can imagine, there is plenty of room on the Maurice and the Walking Rivers for you and your buddy to pole your skiff, should you wish to give that famous area a try for a day or two next seasons. Of course, you can come down to North or South Carolina and book a rail hunt with me, or travel to any of those other rail bird hunting marshes that you're reading about here in *The Rail Bird Hunter's Bible*.

I know a little bit of how the locals feel about their part of southern Jersey, even though I only lived along the New Jersey coast for a few months when I was a young Army officer, then stationed at Ft. Monmouth, New Jersey, for three months in 1985 and two months late in 1990. The locals were mighty nice to me, and I was pleasantly surprised, but the coastal townships are much different from my experiences in Princeton, Trenton, and Atlantic City. Delaware Bay, the Maurice River, and the Walking River rice meadows sure are beautiful rail bird shooting areas, and if you are lucky enough to gun that part of the state's most historic rail bird hunting area, you might consider experiencing each of the greatest rail hunting areas across our great nation during your lifetime. They are all listed in this book.

Each year can be great hunting. I have seen the seasons get better and better with each and every new rail bird season, so don't wait until you are retired to gun these famous rail bird hunting areas. However, do take your time to enjoy the hunt. Savor the surroundings, the marsh, the tides, and the rail birds; be sure to book with a local guide, someone who really knows their way around the hunting area and has been doing it a while; and bring a friend or two with you to share it all whenever you make that outdoor-life adventure in rail bird hunting.

NEW JERSEY RAIL BIRD HUNTING
Wild rice meadows + Sora rail birds = Exceptional marsh bird hunting

Rail bird hunting has been a long-standing tradition in the coastal regions of the Atlantic Flyway—especially so in south Jersey, around the Mauriceville township. Every year for the past century, one unique family of watermen—who are sportsmen in the finest sense of that word—stands out above all other names in the history of New Jersey's coastal family wildfowl hunting history. That would be Camp family, of which members can be found around Port Elizabeth, New Jersey. Many of the Camp family have continued to rail bird guide using their unique, seventy-year-old wooden rail hunting boats, and push/pole their gunners with the same handmade wooden push poles that have been used by scores of that family through the generations. Will that family continue to guide those famed waters for years to come? They hunt and guide in New Jersey's famous wild rice meadows that are grow naturally off the banks of the fresh water Maurice River, which the locals pronounce "Morris" River in their distinct south Jersey tidewater brogue accent.

It is here in the south Jersey coastal community, beginning during the hot and humid month of September's new and full moons and heading well into October's new moon week, especially when northern winds push down chilly-wilily from way up north, that rail birds start gathering and prepare to head south in their early migration. These flocks fly well after the setting sun, and after the full moon rises all that week of October. Flocks migrate during a rail bird "Full Moon Madness" that stirs in these species an inspiration to eat heartily, and start their southward migration. Sora and Virginia rail birds all along the Atlantic Flyway, just as the entire avian community of the northeast coastal inshore marshes, sense the coming of winter within their souls, and something deep within them pushes them to take wing southward.

RAIL BIRD MIGRATIONS

How quickly can the littlest of rail birds migrate, you might ask me? According to USFW bird banding records, retired SC DNR Game Warden Major Ben Moise—who lives in Charleston, South Carolina, and still writes for *Garden* and *Gun* magazines—told me that a "solitary Sora rail bird that was banded in October 1971, under special DNR Fish and Game banding guidelines in Cape May, New Jersey, was killed that next day in Charleston, S.C., and shot in Hamlin Bay, S.C." This banding recovery data shows us just how quickly even the smallest of rail birds can migrate south along the coast to a South Carolina salt marsh, especially when a big ol' northeastern cold front is pushing a flock's little feathered butts southward with fair winds and following seas.

This unique and quick migration of the smallest of marsh birds also happens just prior to the heaviest of storms sweeping onto shore with the heaviest of tides. The King of Tides has been super-storms such as Hurricane Sandy, Hurricane Hugo, and the great storm of 24 August 1814 that hit Washington City and eastern Virginia driving the British Expeditionary Forces out of the U.S. Capital. The Great Storm of October 1888 hit the Atlantic coastal states, bringing a series of tidal wave periods whose flood waters inundated fresh water rivers. Some pushed flood tides all the way up to Albany, New York and Richmond, Virginia, along the James River and the Carolina coastal rivers, after breaking scores of protective dikes that had been built by slave labor over a hundred years prior. This caused salt water to mix in and increase salinity further inland.

These storms virtually destroyed commercial rice growers trying to grow Carolina Gold, who could not recover socio-economically to rebuild their protective dikes built to keep out salt water, due to the high cost of labor following the Reconstruction years.

Hurricanes that hit the coast during the lunar tidal period cause a massive southward migration of the avian migratory community that is rarely seen by human eyes, yet understood by the avian communities' inner nature to get the hell out of Dodge as fast as possible. Their inner senses cause them to take wing and move ever southward before a storm hits. Animals and the migratory community always have that unique "sixth sense"—yet we humans, even when given advanced warning by nature, do not necessary adhere to its wonder. We tarry and get caught up by the devastation of the flood waters from the storm.

Traditionally, rail birds migrate via slower methods of transmigration. However, if a late migration occurs which does happen occasionally due to changes in the jet stream and especially due to warmer throughout the month of August, Sora migrations might leave the Canadian coastal inshore marshes during the full moon in September.

Backcountry Saltmarsh can be quite vast

Therefore, there are times due to milder weather conditions where the migration of very large numbers of a species of rail birds do not move southward out of Canada's Providences until the month of September, then, there are occasions when hundreds of thousands of rail birds might decide to overfly Maine's great wild rice meadows of Merrymeeting Bay, nevertheless, many thousands of Sora's will still stop in the Connecticut River's wild rice to feed heavily for a few days or a few weeks, depending on weather conditions, or other pressures real or imagined, many flocks will continue moving southward, especially the Sora and the King rail, not so much the Clapper, as they may tarry in the saltmarshes all along the Atlantic inshore marshes behind the sea islands until they reach warmer climates in the Carolina's. They will be driven solely by cold fronts or massive NE Storms, which cause them to push southward and occasionally getting caught up pushed to farther inland regions due to the storms of historical significance, as it has all species at various times.

Most of the Atlantic Flyway's rail bird populations might reach Delaware Bay's regional marshes/meadows where the Clapper and the Virginia might gather and disperse in flocks throughout those great marshes all behind the barrier island marshes, after a night or two of migration travel, and the Sora would gather in great flocks (peeping like little chicks) deep within in the wild rice beds, solidly feasting on the wild rice, because it is so nice and stores up energy for their great southern migration to the Delmarva peninsula, the Eastern Virginia marshes, the Patuxent rice fields, VA's famous back Bay, and the Salt marshes of the North Carolina Outer Banks, Core Sound, Neuse River, the Bogue, and the famous Cape Fear onward to the Carolina's, Georgia's marshes, and Northeastern Florida marshes.

This is why sportsmen from throughout the major cities of the Northeastern USA: New York City, Philadelphia, and Washington, D.C., travel by plane, train, and automobile to the unique bayside community of Mauricetown, New Jersey, and for couple of hundred dollars have secured the services of one of the Camp family—or their extended clan of cousins and nephews—who have access to a fleet of Camp family handcrafted wooden rail boat skiffs ready and waiting on a good full flood tide to, hunt rail birds during September and October.

410 SxS rail bird shotgun

A friend of mine from southeastern New Jersey, gunsmith Mr. Darryl Bogart, who's a close friend of Maurice River rail bird guide Walter Camp and his extended family, has been living in New Jersey for most of his natural life, not too far from that great river. I told him that at least four U.S. Presidents have been pushed across the flood waters of the Maurice River by various guides working that special rail bird hunting river for generations. Although Mr. Walter Camp, the oldest member of that illustrious rail bird hunting family, doesn't guide anymore, he certainly stays involved in scheduling hunts for the family's guide business. He has taught his extended family of rail boat guides how to build and maintain a proper rail boat, and push pole sportsmen, and how to properly work the rice meadows, and the tides for pushing their "sports" using the lightest of wooden rail boat skiffs, such as those seen in photos listed in this section of my book.

Darryl first hunted with Mr. Walter way back in September of 1974, and has become quite the rail bird aficionado since day one. Like others who desire to hunt this famed river's rice meadows, he has realized that if you want to hunt the best and highest of tides in southeastern New Jersey's Maurice River, you must lock down one of the last big-name guides of that region, and you have to do it one year in advance in order to get a reservation with one of the Camp family of rail bird guides. They use five rail bird skiffs, most over fifty years old.

All types of people— blue-collar worker and famously well-to-do, wealthy sportsmen alike—come from all the great cities of the Northeast to hunt this section of river and rice in southeastern New Jersey. U.S. Presidents have hunted this most famous of southern New Jersey rail bird hunting rivers. Benjamin Harrison, Grover Cleveland, Col. Theodore Roosevelt, even happy Howard Taft, to name a few important big names, and many other famous sportsmen have booked hunts and gone rail bird hunting when the flood tides and the weather all come together with the most excellent of conditions for just a couple of days each September and October, and the Soras are down in record numbers. President Benjamin Harrison hunted these wild rice meadows well over a century ago. Theodore Roosevelt's first book was on birds, which he finished while still an underclassman at Harvard College. He and his father were likewise drawn to this regional area to hunt rail birds, as was the Philadelphia painter Thomas Eakins. A certain young cousin of Theodore's, Franklin D. Roosevelt himself, hunted rail birds when he was the very young Assistant Secretary of the Navy, then working under President Woodrow Wilson's administration prior to WWI.

Mr. Thomas Eakins painted rail bird hunting scenes at least six times according to art historians, so I've been told. He was inspired, and I have seen a number of them over the years. Down south in Georgia, outdoor writer John Burke, quite a keen ol' rail bird hunter who grew up along the Georgia coast and writes for a number of Georgia outdoors papers and magazines, once told me that President Jimmy Carter went rail bird hunting as a young fellow. Of course, we all know that Jimmy learned to hunt quail and dove down on the farms around Plains, Georgia. I understand that Jimmy had arranged a day to go hunt rail birds down in New Jersey while he was the President of the United States. However, that was also when he was trying to broker that Middle East peace deal between Egypt's President Anwar Sadat and Israel's Prime Minister Menachem Begin, and that situation kept pulling President Carter away from going down to the Jersey coastal inshore waters. Apparently he missed the best tide period—and well, as all you rail bird hunters know…that was the end of that story!

Jimmy had rail bird hunted when he was young fellow a couple of times, but it was Clapper rails that he pursued along the Brunswick island salt marshes, well prior to his entering the U.S. Naval Academy. Since he was a Navy man, I hereby promise to take ol' Jimmy rail bird hunting whenever he finds the time to come down to our coast of North Carolina. Maybe he'll talk Bill Clinton into coming down, too. I understand Mr. Clinton has a mighty nice Winchester Model 21 SxS 20ga quail gun that he hasn't shot much—a gift from when he was governor of Arizona, and I'd certainly like to see him shoot a few railbirds. I don't know if the former Vice President, the Hon. Richard Chaney, feels up to shooting rail birds, as he's not currently in the best of health, and according to my friends in Wyoming he hasn't hunted much as of late. I am not one to talk too much of politics, but I will talk to Mr. Chaney about gun safety when he steps into my rail boat, as I do with all my clients before we go out rail bird hunting on the marsh.

Just what sort of bird can claim the favor of Presidents, and one of America's greatest painters, as well have captains of major industry intertwined with blue-collar New Jersey watermen, poling their wooden skiffs across flooded fields of wild rice meadows? It is not the quail, nor the grouse, nor the wily woodcock. It is, my friends, the littlest of all rail birds hunted today—the Sora rail. A small, chicken-like marsh bird that lofts into the air like a grasshopper, flies like the Wright Brothers, and falls like a stone a split instant before gunners loose the charge of shot that passes, often as not, cleanly over the backs of the birds. In Septembers and Octobers from the 1850s to the 1930s, well over a hundred thousand Soras a year were taken from the marshes flanking the Maurice — most by the 200-odd members of the long-ago disbanded West Jersey Game Protection Society.

On one momentous tide, its members had reported in their Society's hunting journals to have killed 21,000 Sora rail birds — with 365 felled by a single gunner (he must have had a loader) in the boat with him that particular day. But this type of marsh bird hunting certainly died out with the century that spawned such excesses in gunning in that particular marsh. As recorded in the ledgers of southern New Jersey's rail bird guide: Ken Camp hunting operation averaged approximately 1,500 birds a year killed by their gunners over a ten year period according to a interview in 1997. That's an average of approximately ten birds per boat, as they hunt one client and one guide poling during a flood tide push lasting around 90 minutes of solid hunting, before the tides fall and you've got to get off the meadows.

Certainly this bag limit sounds generous, in an age where a single Blackjack (black duck) constitutes that species' legal bag limit, and the Canvasback duck is limited to one. Ken Camp has stated many times that the number of birds killed is quite consistent from year to year. My interviews with Clapper rail bird hunters up and down the Atlantic Flyway show that a personal bag from an average hunt is 8 — 10 birds per person per flood tide. In reflection, in Arkansas, Mississippi Missouri's fresh water marshes, and rice fields the average is 6–8 — Sora rail birds — per hunt period, in these particular environments they will use a one man kayak moving along the edge of these rice field heaver edges or flooded marshes, while- one or two other hunters wade or walk along the edges of marsh grass. This method of rail bird hunting impoundments or shallow marshes are often done with at least one retriever dog moving between the edge of the water and the hunter's walking.

The host of rail birds each fall along the northeast coastal inshore waters, and the harvest in our modern day and time has certainly fallen, as has the number of sportsmen and women that purse rail birds in the New Jersey rice meadows. In all of North America, and especially along the Atlantic Flyway, there are but a handful of coastal areas where rail birds are still hunted in the traditional fashion. Eastern Virginia, southeastern North Carolina, South Carolina, Georgia, and a portion of northeast Florida are areas where an average of 150 to 350 hunters pursues rail birds each year, and some only hunt them a handful of days each year. By comparison, an average duck hunter will hunt 21 days out of a 70-day season, and their bag limits average six birds per state, according to DNR hunting records.

If you are a statical researcher, look at these figures from my survey of one hundred water fowlers and one hundred rail bird hunters over four years of researching this book: waterfowl hunters across the USA (average age: 26 yrs old, with an income level $ +/- 35K) hunt an average of 12 times each duck season, and spend an average of $500 to $1,500 every season. Two duck hunting buddies hunting in the same boat, average six birds every three hunt trips per person across the flyways of America; whereas two rail bird hunters might average 8 to 15 birds, during each hunt trip during a normal flood tide. Each individual rail bird hunter (average age: 55 yrs old, has an average income $60–70K) yet, spends around the same amount per season as the average duck hunter—an average of $500 to $1,500 per season—but rail bird hunters average only two to six flood tide hunt days (4-hour hunts) each season. That is a pretty loyal bunch of rail bird hunters!

In New Jersey, the best area in all of that state's coastal inshore waters is found not far from the southeastern Jersey shore, where rail bird hunting is still going strong to this day. There you will find each and every flood tide that pours into that state's most famous rail bird hunting river during the months of September and October. This would be along the banks of the Maurice River. The author and researcher Robert Mangold in his Migratory

Shore and Upland game birds in North America, written in 1977 states: "Estimates for New Jersey show approximately three thousand rail bird hunters listed fifteen thousand clapper rails." In my New Jersey research I have found that in the past ten years that the public hunting area are still consistent with rail bird migrations in even greater numbers, except for the fall season when Hurricane Sandy hit, when most all species of rail birds moved southward into the Delmar peninsula and the Carolina's.

However my research has shown that most rail bird hunters New York, New Jersey and southeastern Pennsylvania hunt the rice meadows in the northeastern rivers, and theSora rail bird today, more so than the Clapper in the salt marsh meadows. It is a higher bag limit, although the average is certainly much lower- approximately ten Sora's per rail bird hunter on average. This would be over a ten year period of hunters reviewing their personal hunting records or personal journals.

Historical records note that from 1850s until just prior to WWII, the most dominant rail bird hunting areas in the country were the Connecticut River below Essex, with the highest number of rail bird hunters, followed by the Maurice River. In third place were the Patuxent River's rice meadows for Sora rails, followed by the eastern shore salt marshes of Virginia and Maryland. Next in terms of historical numbers of rail bird hunting would be the salt marshes for Clapper rail birds along the North and South Carolina coasts. Serious wildfowlers should strongly consider purchasing an exceptional topo map of your local wildfowling area from MyTopo, which is developed from USGS aerial surveys.

It was primarily Sora rail birds taken throughout the northeast coasts, and the Clapper and Virginia rail birds along the Virginia and Maryland eastern shore saltmarshes. The larger Clapper rails are primarily the rail bird of choice throughout the Carolina coastal salt marshes. Georgia's coastal saltmarshes below the Savannah River's estuary system, also including the wilderness salt marshes along the Brunswick Georgia barrier islands, would be followed in numbers of rail bird hunters by Florida's northeastern salt marsh estuary system. That rounds out the top ten rail bird hunting areas throughout North America—all in the Atlantic Flyway, and in terms of the numbers of hunters that pursue rail bird hunting with a passion every fall.

Most rail bird hunts throughout the Atlantic Flyway are always done by the traditional method, that simply put was hunters taking a light shallow draft skiff out to a marsh where the rail birds are located, and poling the marshes during a high flood tide, with the wind at their backs—which is quite helpful to the guide or poler in moving forward—while the gunner shoots from the bow seat (gunners chair). When hunting tall, thick stands of wild rice, a guide or guide(s) would move all the boats into a great meadow in a parallel line, and push forward through the meadows, thereby ensuring that every gunner in every boat had a good opportunity to shoot rail birds as they jumped.

Safety is tantamount in gunning heavy stands of wild rice, because you can sometimes only see just so far ahead, due to the thickness of the wild rice meadows, therefore I always recommend you to play it safe and you and your buddies should wear orange hats or shirts whenever you are rail bird hunting in such heavy cover. Look closely at the photos of shooting in wild rice. These boats would be about fifty or sixty yards apart, but sometimes they might be closer together, if conditions warrant it, especially when hunting with a group of rail bird hunters on a marsh. Safety is always paramount when pushing through these very vast, tall rice field meadows during rail bird hunting flood tides. Hunting wildfowl in our state's public hunting areas is a privilege not a right, and we rail bird hunters should always be extra careful anytime we are out hunting areas whenever we're hunting wildfowl, and respectful to our fellow sportsmen who are sharing those same hunting areas.

In the middle and northeastern coastal states, most rail bird hunting was done in flooded wild rice meadows along the Potomac, the James River's estuary system, or the salt marshes along Back Bay and eastern Virginia, or Maryland along the coastal saltmarshes and Spartina grass flats. For northeast states, it was while hunting the wild rice meadows in the New Jersey Maurice River, and the Connecticut River, or further northeast along Maine's Merrymeeting Bay and the five major rivers that have stands or meadows of wild rice. In the northeast, it was always during a flood tide period, during the full or new moon's highest of tides in the months of September and October—well before the first major cold fronts push these migratory rail birds further southward. Along the South Atlantic Seaboard coastal inshore waters, they were gunned more in salt marsh Spartina grass flats during flood tides in September through December, depending on the southern states' rail bird seasons that took advantage of split seasons and higher tide days.

Mr. Bob White from Bordertown, Pennsylvania, said: "Each year, around the 15th of September, especially during the full moon week, the rail birds (Soras) would start to appear. They would arrive in great numbers to our rice meadows along the Maurice River. The Susquehanna had beautiful rice meadows too, and people would gun them. Tons of ducks and rail birds were there, but it's all within the city limits and city ordinances forbid the discharging of any firearms inside the city limits." Big houses now line the once-great meadows of the Connecticut River and the Susquehanna.

Said Mr. White, "Lots of the old rice meadows are gone now, when continued dredging deepened the rivers, and more salt is constantly pushing back the fresh water, especially during very high tides, and due to other things, like plants dumping chemicals into the waters. It is just terrible what some businesses will get away with." Nowadays, the EPA will sock it to companies that dump waste into estuaries or rivers, but the damage to the natural resources has been done. Bob told me that each fall, the wild rice meadows (we locals call 'em "meddas") would be plum full of Bobolinks and thousands of Red-winged

Blackbirds, which would always precede the arrival of the Sora rails' migration, all stopping in like a clock on their great southern migration to feed upon the rice meadows. These rail birds would just literally stuff themselves silly with wild rice. It really fattens them all up for their great southern migration—it's the circle of life within the wildfowl community, you know. I had family and friends hunting rail birds all over south Jersey and coastal Pennsylvania since I was a kid, and I'm 74 now, so I'm reflecting back and covering a great deal of waterfowl and wildfowling history."

The Soras would always arrive during the nights of the full moon. If you were not out on the water a lot, you wouldn't realize they had arrived in your favorite river or marsh Said Bob, "It seemed like one day there would be hardly any birds out there in our local rice meadows, and then all of a sudden, they appeared peeping and making noise quite early in the morning. Rails birds back in those days would number well in the thousands or the hundreds of thousands on some meadows, or there might be perhaps hundreds of thousands in the larger 'meddas' that would extend south of the Maurice River bridge., however, I hunted around Philly, until the rice meadows were closed to all hunting due to city ordinances, therefore, I did not start hunting down on the Maurice river until around 1971."

He continued, "I started hunting around the mid 1950s, but even as a young fellow, I would ride my bike down to the docks and see the ferry come in, and the sportsmen would pile off with all their gear, all of 'em talking about going rail bird hunting. September 1 the season would start, but the guides would not start out until the flood tides got very high, then all five boats would guide every day during the week of the high tide in the rice meadows."

Ken Camp had five rail boats, and all were traditional rail bird skiffs for pushing one gunner sitting forward, or standing, through the meadows. His papa and great-grandpapa had guided that same river, so I understand. However, you just couldn't call and get a guide trip with the Camps. One of the regular customers had to drop out or cancel a trip, and if you had been placed on their waiting list, you would get a call, and you had to come on down before that next hunt.

In 1971, professional rail bird guides got $75 to push a sport for one high tide, and you had to include a tip of about $25 to $50. Back in those days, you'd send Ken Camp a check which included the tip. Some of his pushers had their own rail boats, but most of them used one of the five boats the Camps had available. There was one fellow who'd paid for his hunt, but said he "wasn't going out in the rain to hunt," and refused to go hunting that morning, even though it stopped raining later on that same morning and it was coming down good. Afterwards, I heard Ken say that the fellow sleeping in that car would never get invited to hunt with them again. A head guide's got to protect their people, and no refunds are given during rail bird season.

Prices are much higher nowadays, as you can imagine, but it's a welcomed income from a tradition that has continued since the 1850s, when it was first written about in the sporting news papers and magazines of the major U.S. cities. It is still quite loyal a group of hunters, and it's quite strange that there are not more young people hunting today. Perhaps it's just too hard a sport for the young people of today; too much work pushing a light wooden rail skiff through heavy wild rice. There are people who hunt the coastal meadows too, where there are Clappers out on the salt marsh, and I know there must me a couple of million Clappers migrating down the Eastern Seaboard every year.

Bob told me that, "Someone canceled their hunt trip with the Camps, and I got a phone call, as I had asked to be on their stand by hunt list, just in case someone might cancel, and drove down there that next day to hunt with them. It's just a couple of hours' drive from where I live. That's how I got started being guided by the Camp family of rail bird guides, each fall, for seven consecutive seasons during September's full moon's high tide week." I was pretty loyal client, and booked a particular hunt day a year in advance, and hunted with their guide service one hunt each year throughout those years.

"Sometimes I would hunt one extra day during the flood tide week in the month of October too, and it could be just as good, and the weather was not as hot and humid as it normally was in September, however you might get some heavy fronts push through, and those hard winds would extend the high tide and you could hunt longer periods of time. Some Septembers can be mighty warm in southern New Jersey, I tell you! Always depends on the weather, but we always went out. We always enjoyed ourselves, no matter how the hunt turned out, sometimes killing ten or twenty birds, sometimes twenty-five, which is the limit. I never did shoot my limit on a box of shells. I shot an automatic back in those days, but love my 12ga SxS now. It's made by a fellow called Tony Galazan Guns. You should look at his website on the Internet; he also sells classic shotguns, but specializes in Winchester M21s double barrel shotguns. Those are the classic shotguns of the rail bird crowd, a distinct crowd that loves to read *Double Gun Journal* magazine, and *Garden and Gun* magazine."

My first day hunting rail birds, said Bob in thoughtful reflection, "It was pouring down rain, and I drew a guide whom Ken Camp called 'Honk.' Charley Stroman was his real name, and let me tell you, ol' Honk was quite the fellow! He was a mighty strong pusher, always cordial too. In September he'd push barefoot, wearing jeans and an old tee shirt, but he was the nicest fellow you could ever meet. He worked in the New Jersey prison system, like many of the Camps' extended family did, and all of those fellows that pushed for Ken Camp back then were all mighty nice fellows, and good pushers too. They all knew these meadows like the back of their hands, and most all could mark downed rail birds exceptionally well."

Rail bird pushing through wild rice is mighty laborious work, I tell you. I cannot do that anymore, but have some good younger friends who invite me, and I still enjoy shooting the rail birds every September and October during flood tides. There is nothing quite like the Maurice River during a super high tide storm. With what seems like millions of rail birds, it's easy to kill your limit of 25 within an hour. One time back in the 1960s during a Nor'easter, Ken Camp said, "That tide must have stayed high for quite a long time, perhaps two hours, due to northeastern winds, and every boat killed twenty-five Soras per gun, and all the guides on all five boats went across the river with just the guides, and each one of them also killed their limit of rail birds." Yes, sir, said Kenny, that sure was a memorable day for rail bird hunting.

Bob said, "The Camps took over a few generations ago from other guides who used to work the Maurice. Now they are the only professional guides working the Maurice River, and to my knowledge, there are no professional rail bird guides working any of the northeastern state other rivers that have wild rice such as Merrymeeting Bay, in Maine, and of course, the rivers around Philly you cannot hunt rail birds there anymore." I told him that I understand that the wild rice meadows in his old rail bird hunting rivers in southeastern PA are dwindling away, due to dredging, and big homes being built around the rice meadows, and I understand no one is guiding rail bird hunts up on the Connecticut River for a good many years now.

Those were mighty famous, and some had as many as twenty guides operating each river from the 1800s through the Great War. You know, it's still to this day mighty hard to get a open date for a rail bird hunt on the Maurice River, as the Camps get booked up fast, and it's all word–of–mouth within the waterfowling community throughout the great cities of the northeastern states. David Miller from northeastern New Jersey commented, "All the major cities are a close journey to the Maurice River: Trenton, NYC, Philly, and Atlantic City. There are lots of wealthy sportsmen who continue to come down to Mauricetown and the surrounding riverside community to be guided by the Camp family of rail bird guides. They are now run by young Kenny Camp Jr. You can see him in those photos that I've sent you for your NJ section of your book. These hunts with friends and family are annual events book a year in advance, and are all wonderful hunting memories, however, I have always wanted to come down south and hunt the southeastern coastal marshes for Clapper rail birds, and I hope to do that more now that I have more time to travel and hunt."

Bob White mentioned to me that, "I ended up buying one of the Camp guide's personal rail boat from Ol' 'Honk' after he guided me for seven seasons, and stopped guiding. That boat was originally built back in the war years, but boy was he proud of his old rail bird skiff, always keeping it in exceptional condition! I then hunted with friends all over southern New Jersey, and up in Maine's rivers too, but there is nothing that really compares with the Maurice River rice meadows, and the beauty of that wonderful rail bird hunting area in this part of the nation. I love hunting rail birds in the traditional manner, pushing your skiff that you keep it shipshape, and enjoy poling it. Yes, it can be mighty hard work when the rice is tall and strong, but this is a unique gentleman's hunting and it's not done in a lot of states or regions around our nation, but here on the coastal inshore, it's quite beautiful, and you know there are hundreds and thousands of wildfowlers, across our nation who really do not realize what kind of exciting gunning they are missing out."

J.P. Hand wrote me these words about his experiences out rail bird hunting since the 1950s: "I appreciate and respect all those who've shown me kindness over the years, and the friendships I've made over the years of my life throughout the rivers and meadows, the wonderful sunrises and the sunsets I've experienced throughout my life, and have been blessed to share with a great many young and old outdoorsmen throughout my life. Wildfowlers know this feeling—it's deep within our hearts, our minds, and our very souls. Others, who have never experienced such things, find it hard to grasp the many small and large aspects that develop throughout the course of a day or morning in the Great Outdoors."

A light canoe works well in rail bird hunting, especially when the wind isn't bad

CHAPTER NINE

Middle Atlantic States: Maryland, Delaware, Virginia

Maryland, Delaware and Virginia's famous wildfowl hunting areas in the marshes are just as productive as the rich farming lands of Easton, where Canada geese are the number one waterfowl hunted today. For rail bird territory, look to the marshes off the Delmar historic regional wildfowling areas: Chesapeake Bay, Delaware Bay, Nanticoke River and Marshyhope River delta marshes, as well as the Rebouth and Indian River tidal marshes. Eastern Maryland's historic wildfowling in the Assateague bays and marshes are quite diverse, and there are local guides that can take you after rail birds.

Marsh hens can be found throughout eastern Virginia's Pocomoke Sound, and the marshes around Lewisetta, Lilian, Mobjack, and marshes behind Plum Tree Island, at flood tides (remember, always keep abreast of tides and the DNR-FW regulations). These grand wildfowling areas are still a wildfowler's dream, where a ton of Clapper rails abound. You should lock in your local rail bird guide well in advance, if you want him to push the marshes during September and October's highest of flood tides.

Other rail bird areas are found in a dizzying array of marshes, if you have a light skiff and a push pole, and a loyal Labrador or Chessie to retrieve your kill. You will want to concentrate on new and full moon flood tides, and push through in your kayak, skiff, or Jon boat in the back marshes and bays off Chincoteague, Wachapreague, Quimby, or Hog Island Bay, and the Cobb Island salt marshes. These are most unusual and beautiful wilderness wildfowl hunting areas, with Native American names reflecting periods of history that are not forgotten in those local communities.

South Bay or Back Bay's marsh complex has its great estuary Spartina artaflosia salt marshes, where marshes and creeks abound, and rail birds and wildfowl are most abundant in massive numbers in September and October, and more so after a hard Nor'easter pushes down southward in October or early November, before rail bird season ends.

These historic Eastern Virginia rail bird hunting areas are traditionally rich in natural resources as they are in wildfowl. Anyone who hunts and fishes in eastern Virginia realizes that there has been problems with environmental issues related to run off problems, farming, etc…however, there has been a great deal of environmental research that continues to be done to keep the environment in check, especially in the marshes and rivers of eastern Virginia, Chincoteague, Cape Charles, and the region's historic rivers: the Patuxent, Potomac, and James rivers. *Rallidae* still push down by the hundreds, thousands and throughout a fall migration millions of birds visit, feed, and move southward as all rail bird species migrate each fall along the Eastern Seaboard's Atlantic Flyway, from breeding grounds way up north in the Boreal marshes of James Bay and the Maritime Island marshes, where they are lightly hunted, if hunted at all by Canadian wildfowlers—who seem much too busy deer hunting in September and October to bother hunting marsh birds or wildfowl. They certainly do not realize what great hunting they are missing when they are not out on the marsh during rail bird season.

All along these eastern shore marshes, you will be amazed by miles and miles of shallow and deep muddy oyster-filled bays, teeming with blue crabs, shrimp, and sporting fish. Fresh water streams run and empty into salt marsh estuaries, still bountiful and blessed with oysters and crabs since the days of early settlers along those then-Colonial coastal regions, townships and fishing villages. Is there any wonder that many residents were still loyal to King George III well after the Revolutionary War years? Here you will find many tight-knitted coastal towns, families and communities that depend upon their friends and neighbors, and the sea and the marshes, for their bounty and natural resources.

It wasn't until well into the Industrial Revolution years that modern improvements and wealthy sportsmen moved into these tidewater regions, which had always seen their share of ships and traders pass by throughout the years. Here you will still find a peaceful and temperate community of tight-knit watermen, and families and areas quite diverse ecologically. The back country wilderness marshes are diverse and massive—a casual glance on Google Earth will easily show you just how much wilderness back country there is throughout this region. Flood tides bring freshness and life, and if you are present, just keep your eyes open long enough. You can certainly see for yourself the abundance of natural resources that can be found through all of eastern Virginia.

Waterfowling history was certainly very rich in those early years, as our nation developed from an agricultural into an industrial community. In that light, there was more money and more pleasures to be obtained. Many different hunting and fishing clubs sprung forth from counties throughout these particular tidewater regions, communities, and fishing towns, whose generations of watermen took from its waters and marshes millions of wildfowl, crab, and oyster throughout the centuries.

A quick look at the older coastal village communities that sprung up all along the eastern Maryland and eastern Virginia tidewater regions still link families, now long gone, from those regions. However, unique and beautiful communities are waiting for you to explore. Consider places like Long Neck, Chestertown, Bryanttown, Romancoke, Tilghman and Taylor's Island, Hoopersville, Elliotte, Wenona, Crisfield, and Cobb Island, whose residents, sporting visitors, and watermen got into wildfowling. Local guides took wealthy "sports" out hunting and fishing to make more cash in the poorer fishing and whaling communities that took root along barrier islands. Some of these areas were not really civilized until well after the Revolutionary War ended, and more families and towns did indeed spring forth, and more fishing villages were established across the rich tidewater region. This came well after the War of 1812, when our nation felt the sting of British sailors and Royal Marines raiding coastal whaling and fishing villages from Delaware south along the Outer Banks, all the way to Spanish Florida.

When great hunting lodges were established along the coastal inshore by wealthy northerners, locals were put to work as labors, paddlers, and cooks. Some spouses also took in extra cash cooking and cleaning wild game, as well as working in new industries that later came to this unique community. Greenbacks flowed mightily into these tidewater communities, providing jobs and finances that were much needed in what for many had been a struggling coastal commercial fishing industry, where men earn their daily bread by tonguing for oysters, crabbing, and shrimping. There were fishing villages big and small, where many families have continued for generations to work these waters to this day, as their father's fathers did, and will for many generations to come.

Rail bird hunting was always done the traditional way along the fresh water and salt marshes dominated by the flood tides, as wild rice abounded in the fresh water rivers and throughout the massive acres of salt marshes—but mostly during the super high tides of September and October's full and new moon weeks, when tides ran at their highest peak. However, it was certainly not in great numbers, and there was very little value in market gunning rail birds during its heyday of the 1850s to 1918. This was due to the difficulty of getting at these rail bird species, but more so due to the smaller size of the marsh birds. Restaurants paid top dollar for wildfowl, mostly wanting what "well-paying customers" desired to feast upon, like Canvasback and Brant. People loved to feast on roasted wild duck and goose breasts, and shops served steaming bowls of Terrapin Stew and good cuts of beef, rather than just pork and venison, to well-paying customers of those days and times.

There was a growing market for other marsh birds, such as the Sooty Turn and the Spanish Piper, but it was mostly for their feathers, which almost decimated certain species due to the growing demand of changing social styles for the modern woman of the day. There was a growing demand for feather hats among the fashionably dressed women of that time and era.

The waterfowling that developed along eastern Maryland had always been excellent, but changes occurred throughout the late 1840s and well into the 1850s, and as our nation's economic systems took a hit due to captains of industry building economic kingdoms, locals learned quickly that more money could be obtained guiding sports. Market gunning quickly developed, and business flourished, as did many sleepy tidewater towns and communities—primarily due to the shipping of thousands upon thousands of barrels of ducks, geese, swan, and Brant into the marketplace, as well as tons of oysters and blue crab by wagon, and by sailboat. Later, faster delivery came about with more steamers and refrigerated cars, pulled by trains that bounded off to the major cities and larger port towns all along the Northeast.

Delaware's tidewater residents also got into market gunning, as did Virginia's tidewater marshes and the famous areas such as Chincoteague, Assatigue Bays and marshes, and eastern Virginia's famous Potomac and Patuxent Rivers' wild rice meadows. There was some wild rice well above the James River's tidal marshes, and those wonderful Back Bay salt marshes have creeks and bays and vast marshes that are home to so many natural resources, and teeming with wildfowl.

Today you will find some excellent rail gunning in the Maryland marshes off Choptank, the Tangier Sound Marshes, and the back bay marshes of Assateague, accessible only during floodtides. However, much better rail bird hunting can be found throughout eastern Virginia's salt marshes off Chincoteague, where you can obtain a local guide to take you out on high tide days. I would not recommend that you waste your valuable time trying to walk up rails during the incoming tide, unless you are a bear for hard and dangerous wading in the muck of that region's marsh areas. Contact the Maryland and Virginia DNR for up-to-date regulations, and the locations of public landings, public hunting areas, and the many different WMAs that you might have available near you, which may be open for hunting rail birds in tidal areas.

There are also those vast marshes of Wachapreague. Eastern Virginia's rail bird hunting guru, John Shtogren, calls this region the "Rail Hunting Mecca of Eastern Virginia." Having been stationed in Norfolk, Virginia Beach, and Little Creek, Virginia, over the years, I certainly know those areas, and you can see for yourself just how vast those marshes really are when you first take a hard look at them. These famous rail bird hunting areas are open and available for the gentleman rail gunner who can trailer an outboard and a light skiff, and has a hearty back for push poling that skiff through the marsh during a high flood tide, should you choose to go during the new or full moon high tidal days of September and October when the rail bird seasons are open. Some of the southern states rail bird seasons run into the month of December. You should get over into your local saltmarshes in the spring months to do some fly fishing and get to know how to pole those flats well prior to the rail bird season—and to watch your tides!

Father and Son

Good Form with a 20ga OU–Clapper rail bird jumps forward (S.Bennett photo)

Rustin from Oregon–1st Clapper rail–Cape Roman NWR, S.C. special rail bird hunt

Swinging on a railbird

CHAPTER TEN

SOUTHEASTERN REGION: North Carolina, South Carolina, Georgia, and Florida

It is here in these inshore coastal areas of the Atlantic Flyway where one will find the greatest numbers of rail bird hunters during the flood tidal periods than in any other state in the U.S.

The semi-dural tides impacting these inshore tidal saltmarshes can be quite impressive: Savanna, Georgia's Estuary's has nine-foot tides in October, you will find high eight foot flood tides down in Beaufort, S.C., and in Charleston, S.C. a 6.7 H/T is mighty high flood tide, however along the Lower Cape Fear delta marshes of North Carolina- a 5.8 flood tide is about as high as it gets, unless a northeastern front hits during a full moon week during rail bird season. Those massive salt marsh that lie behind the barrier islands of these coastal inshore marshes, certainly do allow for more effective gunning for those seeking to flush out rail birds through poling these backcountry marshes, and this is certainly due to the great flood waters that occur in each of these states' coastal salt marshes throughout the new moon and full moon flood tide periods from September to December. South Carolina currently has a split season that allows rail bird hunting in the month of December's highest tides.

There is plenty of public hunting available in each state's public coastal waters. All you need is a light skiff drawing less than six inches of draft, with a strong heart and shoulders for poling, and a good set of eyes and a steady hand, for gunning the flood tidal periods of these inshore waters when the flood tide rises, slowly flushing the rail birds out of the thickest salt marsh, which is their primary habitat. Some will have started evacuating their marshes due to the flooding to seek higher ground and thicker cover, if there is higher ground to be found. Any keen observer will notice the birds as the wise, older adult rails begin running and flying as the tide moves higher, and as hiding places get slimmer for even the skinniest of rail birds.

For those birders and hunters seeking out these birds in their native marsh habitat, it is the coastal inshore waters that provide primary shelter to the majority of these species of Rail birds throughout their migratory period, since the beginning of time when they evolved as a species. In the winter the clapper rail winters in estuaries in the southeastern marshes near the coast, however some are found far inland too, I have seen them in marsh areas off the Roanoke and off the NE Cape Fear, into the James river in VA, and up the Patuxent, a number of Clappers were seen in Cape May New Jersey Saltmarshes by duck hunters wintering over in small numbers by duck hunters who jumped them and watched them fly away. These are not cripples, that have to remain in northern marshes as many wildfowl biologists and researchers such as the likes of Roth, Meanly, Stewart, or like I have wondered, as to just why would some numbers of clappers desire to stay up north in the freezing and coldest months of December and January in those saltmarshes of Cape May County, N.J., obviously some numbers have obviously done so, but still the majority of rail birds have migrated to warmer climates southwards months ago.

I was at that tender year of learning to shoot a single-barrel Stevens twenty-gauge shotgun when I got the opportunity to shoot at and miss my first rail, when I was not yet eight years old. My mama and papa felt that their freckled-face boy was old enough to travel with friends of the family who were medical doctors at the Medical University of South Carolina (MUSC), and have a go with the rail birds during a flood tide in the year 1966. It was a time of great excitement, and we all had a jolly good time hunting those clapper rail birds.

I remember that I got nice sunburn, regardless of the copious amounts of Coppertone suntan lotion my mama lathered on my face and neck. I remember the push poler's name—it was Mr. Thomas T. Tomilin, who seemed about 70 years old, with a weathered face cut by years and hours of salt life, spent on a shrimping boat, and years in the outdoors cropping tobacco, and working with row crops, and traveling around the world, he told me about visiting Paris in 1918 when he served as an infantryman with Black Jack Pershing's Americal Division with the U.S. AEF in WWI. His roots came from around Hamlin Sound, and his wife, the cheerful Annie Mae, once showed me how she would weave marsh grass, and said that she had kin back in West Africa who were princes and princesses centuries ago. What an education was available to young people willing to learn about these waters, if we are only willing to ask questions, listen, and learn from our elders.

It seemed to me that although he had never been educated beyond the sixth grade, Mr. Thomas was more knowledgeable than any great outdoorsman. The likes of Ernest Hemingway, Robert Rourke, and Nash Buckingham could never learn as much about hunting these elusive rail birds on the Carolina coastal salt marsh, as Thomas could teach me. Some days I was dropped off at his house, where they had raised three children who went on their separate ways. His old house—where I enjoyed grilled rail breasts stuffed with oysters and wild rice, diced onions and mixed vegetables, corn on the cob, and some of the sweetest iced tea that you'd ever tasted, and Mrs. Annie would make a sweet potato pie, or sometimes there were a pile of big ol' hog head scratched biscuits "dis side of heaven"—was demolished back in the late 1970s. None of his children live in the Carolinas any more. They all moved to larger cities upcountry, or further north in New York City and Baltimore. He taught me how to pole a skiff, to make it move to the port or the starboard side, he was a mighty fine teacher.

Although some local rail birds may be around in early September, and a mere handful of rail birds might have been pushed down from way up north in Jersey's marsh and inshore meadows, or the Middle Atlantic marshes, however most of the Sora and Kings as well as Virginia will not move south unless first pressured by heavy gunning, or very cold fronts pushing through, and the occasional massive storm or hurricane that might hit nearby. A lot of local marsh hens or clapper rail populations from New York's saltmarshes, Jersey's Spartina meadows, or Maryland's and Virginia's East Bay marsh complexes, will winter over somewhere along the Atlantic coastal saltmarshes from North Carolina southward to northeastern Florida's Fernanda marsh complexes, as well as the complex inshore brackish waters of the Indian River and Banana River saltmarshes near Cape Canaveral.

Some rail birds do not linger much between banding dates and get down south as quickly as their little wings can take them. How quickly, you might inquire? There was a Clapper banded in Chincoteague on 26 August 1950, killed by a rail bird hunter and reported killed near the Amelia Island, Florida, marshes on 24 September 1950.

There was a Sora rail bird banded on a day prior to the full moon of October 1971, which was killed the next day in a wilderness marsh northeast of Charleston, S.C. Even the most cynical readers must have to admit that's some serious flying, for a little rail bird like a sora to cover in such a short period of time.

RAIL HUNTERS WHO LATER IN LIFE BECAME QUITE FAMOUS

Major General Julian C. Smith, USMC, grew up in Elkton, Maryland. He never got into the fighting during WWI, although he was awarded the Medal of Honor (MOH) in the Banana Wars in Haiti, where he served with Chesty Puller, who grew up in Virginia.

General Smith was a fine old Southern gentleman of fine moral fiber! He had a general love for his people, and his Marines. Smith notes, "I'm a old rail bird shooter from the marshes of Chesapeake Bay, where you pole your wooden skiff rail boat up onto the marshes with the wind at your back, and pole into the salt marsh grass flats and flush out rail birds with the flooding neap tide of September and October during the full and new moon's highest of tides."

General Julian's experiences were in amphibious warfare, with the use of shallow draft amphibious boats needed to land thousands of FMF Marines against the Japanese forces that had dug into the islands of the Pacific. He took on the reins of the famous 2d Marine Division in WWII prior to the landing on Tarawa in the Gilberts. He had the intuition to pick the MOH winner, Colonel Edison of Marine Raider fame, to be on his staff. Edison was another great combat fighter who cut his teeth out in the salt marshes of eastern Virginia's Back Bay and Assateague marshes as a rail hunter, as well as back in the farms of Virginia in the briars and soybean fields as a quail hunter of some distinction.

They made a excellent team. Smith was the great planner and visionary. They got another hunter: David Monroe Shoup, then a 38-year-old Lt Colonel, and when in receipt of orders was a Lt Co in the FMF. General John R. Allen, USMC (Ret), once told me a story about Shoup. General Allen was, back in the spring of 1994, my Lt Colonel with 2d Battalion, 4th Marines. He said, "There is no near miss in amphibious warfare; and Shoup's life was almost cut short a number of times in night attacks on Guadalcanal, when he served with the Old Breed as an artillery observer. However, he was a squat, red-faced man, a Marine's Marine, and an officer and a gentleman who was the brainiest, coolest Marine many had ever met."

Fate had much in store for these Marines. Yet it was Shoup's and Smith's years out in the salt marsh rail hunting where they first cut their teeth on understanding the complexities of high tides, and the sport of hunting marsh hens, and about what a shallow draft boat can accomplish in helping any gunner accomplish an objective. Shoop was earlier the Captain of the USMC Rifle Team, and would go one to become the only living Marine to win the MOH at Tarawa. All men worked tirelessly to ensure that those qualified will be ready to do what is necessary to get any job completed. Lessons learned in the days of their youth, as they enjoyed time well spent in the rail boat.

I remember now a nice, warm September hunt along the salt marsh in eastern Virginia. We killed two limits of Clappers within a two-hour flood tide, and it was now falling as we moved to a shallow creek. The birds that had proved so easy to find during the peak of the high tide, would quickly become quite elusive, and their constant laughing call—kak, kak, kak—would help provide some indication of just how many hundreds, if not thousands of rail birds might be hiding in the tall marsh grass all around us. The phrase "thin as a rail" refers to just how easily rail birds can slip around grass reeds, in order to hide deep in the salt marsh. My father, LtCol J.G. Dinkins Jr., (AUS Ret), used to say this about hunting Clapper rails:

"Unlike shooting other types of waterfowl, marsh birds are really wildfowl, and as webless migratory wildfowl they need to be studied more as a species. Marsh hens are mighty fun to hunt. They can swim just as fast as any Green Wing Teal, and probably swim faster than teal birds. I can tell you from forty-five years of hunting experience that rail birds are great tasting (similar to quail), and they are mighty sporty fliers, especially with 14- to 20-knot winds pushing their striped butts through the sky."

THE ATLANTIC KING AND CLAPPER

Alexander Wilson, the great early Philadelphia Ornithologist whom Audubon referenced occasionally, felt that the Clapper and the King Rail bird to be one and the same, just that Wilson felt the king was the adult when studying in Great egg harbor, New Jersey. It was Audubon's good friend the Reverend Dr. John Bachman that actually studied each species and pointed out that although they are the similar, they are not the same, and it was Audubon in his 1835 journal account discusses this aspect more in detail in his dissertation on these two species.

The Clapper is prolific to say the least, and it's a dominate migrator as well. A Clapper rail bird banded on 7 August 1951 in Chincoteague was killed off Brunswick Estuary's great salt marsh complex in September of that same year. One of the two Clapper rail birds that were banded in New Jersey during the breeding season that same year, was caught in a trap in South Carolina on the 14th of September, while another was reported captured outside the Savannah, Georgia estuary system by researchers allied with UGA and GA DNR, in a joint banding program on the 14th of September 1951.

Sora rail can reach speeds of in excess of 30 mph without a windy day, as you can see for yourself on my YouTube (Joe Guide Sora rail) hunting video. Unlike shooting other types of migratory mars h birds, the best sport with Clapper and Sora rails has very little to do with opening day hunts. Unless there is a full or a new moon high tide, you might as well do some yard work, go fishing, or stay at home.

Wading for rail is quite dangerous in any tidal salt marsh environment, and that soft "puff mud" has caused many a person who thinks they can jump up some marsh hens in their local marsh to forget that way of hunting them ever again—especially when they have to call for help on their personal cell phones for a good friend or the local USCG to come rescue them, because they are stuck waist-deep in the marsh mud. The traditional method of hunting marsh hens is properly done with a push pole, a shallow draft boat, and a good strong pair of shoulders pushing the gentleman sport, who is sitting up front on the gunner's seat, through a flood tide in a salt marsh flat, which are mostly located well behind the barrier islands all along the Atlantic Coast.

Remember, no use of power (electric or outboard) is allowed in pursuit of Rallidae! With a strong breeze at your back, you and your hunting partner can let the wind become your friend, and can take turns poling, and share the time of the highest flood tide at the gunner seat in the front chair of your skiff. Of course, you can also hire a guide to do your poling, so you can enjoy the shooting all to yourself.

Therefore, rail hunters along the Atlantic Coast will certainly need a good local tide chart, so you can determine exactly when the highest of the full or new moon high tides will occur in your part of the coast. It wouldn't hurt to pray for a good Nor'easter, or southeastern winds along the Atlantic Flyway's coastal inshore salt marsh to help the highest of high tides flood your salt marsh, in order to pursue rail birds during the season. There are some mighty fine rail bird hunting marshes all along the Atlantic Flyway, and more specific areas you should look at more closely before planning a rail bird hunting trip.

There are many people who are quite successful during these very high tides who bring out kayaks on their big skiffs, and anchor their boats upwind of a big Spartina flat, and paddle their kayaks while hunting marsh hens. This has become more popular over the years. Kayakers use the wind as their friend in gunning rails in the salt marsh during flood tides. This has also become quite popular for hunting rail on flooded rice fields, and in fresh water marshy lakes and reservoirs that allow hunting, such as those that can be found in Minnesota, Wisconsin, the Central Flyway, or some of the shallow-water lake marshes in Wyoming and Missouri, or in Montana's Freezeout Lake in September and October. However, the rail birds may not stay for long on marshy lakes such as those, due to the cold fronts pushing down from Canada.

A lot of locals tend to overlook those shallow water marshes and impoundments, as well as marshy lakes and private rice fields that they can gain permission to hunt for September or October rail birds during their migration from Canada's great marshes in their Central Flyway push southward. You will never know what marsh hen hunting is like in your part of the nation, until you actually get out there and scout during those fall months, in your kayak or shallow draft boat, and pole the marsh or the rice fields, and shoot some rail birds once they start migrating down from up north.

Any first-time marsh hen hunters, who experience their first traditional rail bird hunt in gunning these birds at the best of times and highest tides, will find that these migratory birds can provide you with some of the fastest legal bird shooting that still remains in the United States of America. Clapper rail birds provide some super exciting hunting with 15-bird limits, and in the northeast you'll find 25-bird limits and exceptional table fare. These, my friends, are more than a few reasons to plan on booking a rail bird hunt on the high super tides during the months of September and October. In South Carolina, their season runs into December, as more birds will not come down until later in November. There are some 6.5 to 6.8-foot tides outside of Charleston, and some 8.5 to 9-foot H/T down along the Savannah coast.

What are you waiting for, a personal invitation? You need to book a trip as soon as you can, for a full moon week, super high rail bird tide, and get it written down on your future plans calendar in big red letters: **GONE RAIL BIRD HUNTING!**

In October, more rails will migrate south along the Flyway as hard frost, and a series of cold fronts hit "up north" along the northeast coast brings hundreds of thousands, if not millions of rail birds migrating down south. While I was a post graduate student at DRMI at the Naval Post Graduate School in Monterey, California, I got to read David A. Adams and Thomas L. Quay's Master's thesis, *"Ecology of the Clapper Rail in Southeastern North Carolina"*. You may obtain a copy of their 1957 research thesis for that senior author in partial fulfillment of his Master of Science degree in Zoology, which he obtained in January 1957. You could obtain a copy for a fee via the North Carolina State College, which is in Raleigh, N.C. You would find it most interesting reading if you enjoy wildfowl biology and statistical research about the clapper rail (Rallus longirostris) as much as I do.

In cleaning a lot of rail birds over forty years of hunting clappers, soras, kings and soras their stomachs will tell me a great many things will have eaten many different invertebrates, and clams, and you have already read how much the Sora and King will love fresh water marshes, and invariably a limited number of those two species will inhabit the brackish water marshes along with the clapper rail. History show us that soras love to chow down on wild rice throughout their migration along the northeastern and Mississippi flyways inshore waters and rivers, as well as the flooded rice field impoundments as well; however, in the salt marshes, of the Atlantic Flyway, and the Gulf states, the Clapper rail will eat three primary food sources: fiddler crabs, spartina snails (periwinkles), and marsh grasshoppers. They will resort to eating worms, as well as clams, and insects too.

What has really changed since the first article ever written on marsh hen hunting? In 1853, John Krider and H. Milnor Knapp described rail hunting along the New Jersey wild rice meadows, and it really hasn't changed much throughout the years—except there are now hundreds of thousands, if not millions more rail birds migrating down along the Atlantic Flyway from up north than in that day. The old wild rice fields along the Connecticut River are pressured more by million-dollar homes looking out majestically across the rice meadows, and fewer and fewer numbers of hunters come to Essex, Connecticut to gun along the great wild rice meadows nowadays.

Today you will find that the Sora rail birds still migrate down and stopover in Connecticut River's rice meadows in the tens of thousands; some stay a week or two, and move southward, other flocks move in and fresh numbers will appear each week, until that last week of the full moon in October, yet, how long they remain in a given area, really depends on the weather conditions, and the food sources. However, there are fewer hunters out there in those meadows pursuing them during highest of high tide days in the marsh. New Jersey had, as of the fall in the year 1928, twenty professional rail guides that were "registered guides" available for hunters to hire for a half-day's adventure in the great rice meadows, or further out on the Delaware Bay salt marsh, where the larger Clapper rails are located.

Prices back as late as 1875 got to be an amazing $5 to $10 to hire a experienced guide to push his wooden skiff for a couple of hours in the tidal marsh, or in a fresh water rice meadow. Even with a liberal 25 Sora rail birds per person, it still is today some excellent hunting during very high full moon tides in Maine or New Jersey in this century, and it takes about six Sora breasts in order to bake those little rail bosoms deep into a "peep pie": Just add some cut potato, onion, and some diced vegetables. I'll talk about that in the recipe section of this book. Of course you can soak a large number of sora breasts in a mixture of wine, and diced onion, salt and pepper and grill up some sora nuggets. Now, that's some good eating! You may have never heard of a Peep Pie before today, but you just try it, and I know you'll like it. They taste just like quail.

From the 1850s to 1917 along the Atlantic coastal saltmarshes, there was excellent rail gunning, but beginning around the 1880s fewer rail bird guides were not available to pole their sports. This was due to the rise in watermen and guides that get into market gunning for waterfowl, which was still going strong during that particular time period. More money was to be made on big waterfowl breasts shipped to restaurants in the big northern cities, which paid top dollar for some species of waterfowl. There was not much of a market for the little rail birds, so they were not heavily impacted by the market gunners of that time—although locals along all the barrier islands along the South Atlantic coast caused some damage while "going egging" among the nesting Rallidae, called "marsh hens" by the locals. It was a matter of being poor and growing up along the coastal salt marsh, and also about good eating.

Lots of things in hunting were discontinued when the 1918 Federal Game Bird laws came into effect. Of course, the coastal folks were also into eating sea turtles and sea turtle eggs all along the Eastern Seaboard islands, and it would be a number of years before federal laws started protecting sea turtles along the coast. Those barrier islands were also protected from development, and natural resources such as shore birds, gulls, bitterns, and sea turtles helped to stop market gunning. The destruction of sea turtles finally drew attention, and serious fines were leveled and articles written about these things. Life continues along the coastal inshore waters, and the people are more educated now. Protecting sea turtles is mighty big business nowadays, with Hollywood, the media, and environmentalists establishing a lot of protections and sanctuaries for nesting sea turtles, and turtle hospitals drawing lots of tourists dollars. It makes a lot of sense to capitalize on these natural resources, with the positive impact of tourism dollars to see and experience unique outdoors areas and hunting opportunities which are part of our southern coastal heritage.

Further southeast in the large salt marshes of the low country, along the cities of Wilmington, North Carolina, and down in South Carolina's wildfowl coastal hunting areas of Georgetown, Charleston, and the Edisto, and Combahee Rivers, rail hunting was a great sport. There were a lot of Northerners and their guests who came south for the early fall to spend their winters along the coastal states. Further south along Georgia's barrier islands, there are some serious nine-foot high tides come September and October, and rail hunting is mighty fine shooting south of Savannah, along Brunswick Sea Island salt marshes, and off St. Mary's, Georgia. You can find good rail hunting in October and November down in northeast Florida behind Amelia Island salt marshes, and off the Indian River estuary system during the highest of high tides.

Now, there are opportunities to rail bird hunt in certain WMA areas on limited days and time periods throughout the rail bird seasons. Many hunters take advantage of gunning for rail birds and experiencing some of the wilderness areas that their parents' and grandparents' tax dollars paid to establish. This is something new that wasn't available back when I was a young man.

A good marsh hen guide/paddler might cost you different amounts for their services. Depending on where you were hunting, it was good money for some hard poling—around $ 1 to $3 dollars a tide back in the 1850s until just prior to the Civil War. From around 1868 to the 1870s, there were more guides operating along the northeast rivers and rice meadows for the wealthy sports from the big cities, who paid a ten-dollar gold piece to push one tide. The tips in the off-season could equal a guide's monthly salary.

From the 1880s to 1920s, guide fees would run from $10 to a $20 gold piece per tide, and more if the guide owned his own rail boat. Some guide services prided themselves on their expertise, and others allied themselves with big hotels, and serviced the sports and their families in package deals. There were always knowledgeable guides to push sports through the rice meadows of rivers and communities within two hours travel from all the major cities of the Northeastern U.S. These were exceptional wages for that time period, and for the local waterman, who prided themselves on their strength and their knowledge of the rice meadows, and keeping up with the wildfowl,

You can therefore see just why, there were more railbird guides and special boats made for the rice field meadows along rivers from Maine through Jersey, as these hunting areas became more accessible via railroad. More and more coastal communities sought to obtain sporting visitors. It was big business to a great number of communities throughout the Eastern Seaboard states, but especially so along the coastal inshore waters.

Times changed through the years, and the Depression cut deeply into this sport. However, the wealthy elite still went railbird shooting each September and October, and there were lots of people who lived along the Atlantic Coast inshore waters who were greatly appreciative of any monies coming in throughout the 1930s to the WWII years, when things changed again. Times have changed over the years, but the little Sora rail birds migrate each full moon period in the thousands and the hundreds of thousands, preceding most cold fronts that start pushing down from Canada's provinces. They do not tarry for long in the Boreal marshes, but move quickly into moonlit nights, fluttering along their travels ever southward, lingering long enough to fatten themselves on rice seed before taking wing once again with the winds.

Doctor W.W. Volletton, M.D, took my father and me on our very first rail bird hunt. We paid $20 for a gentleman named Mr. Thomas Tomlin to push our wooden skiff during that hunt. Mr. Thomas was quite the character, as his background was Gullah accent, but he loved the salt marsh as dear as life itself. The full moon was mighty pretty during that early morning drive to the coast. It was the week of the October's full moon and it was a fantastic rail bird flood tide in 1968, when we hunted outside Charleston. We hunted the marshes off James and John's Island, and later hunted the marshes off the Cooper and the Edisto River marshes near Yellow House Creek. Sometimes we would go rail bird hunting during a day when a cold front hit, and the winds were pushing that tide mighty damn higher than normal, and we always had excellent gunning for rail birds along the spartina grass flats along the historic brackish waters of the Cooper River.

Times certainly have changed a great deal over the years I have been hunting marsh hens , as now a good guide will cost you today approximately $350 to $400 for a half day (4-hr trip) per person, depending on exactly where you are hunting rail birds from Maine to Florida along the Atlantic Flyway. Some guides in coastal Georgia can be found for around $300 for a flood tide period, and these will be hunting the great Savannah estuary system, which incudes your round trip to the hunting marshes from the landing. Be sure that your guide is USCG certified, and shows their certification to you. Many states also register their guides, as my state does. In New Jersey, rail bird guides do not need to be USCG Certified if they're not using outboards. However, they certainly do in many other states across the U.S. when they are hunting or fishing. You can find out those regulations via your own state's DNR.

My grandmother had a cousin who lived on a old plantation below Savannah, Georgia and one of her workers took me out rail bird hunting in the late 1970s, and we did some red fishing on our way back to the boat landing. Beautiful marshes are down there, and when I lived in Georgia in the mid eighties I had friends stationed out of the Naval Station at St. Mary's, Georgia, and, I use to chase Clappers down around the salt marshes there in the very high tides of September and October, but they had large bay boats and we couldn't get out too far except on the highest of tides, we were always afraid of getting stuck out on the marsh back in those days. The rail birds are just as numerous as they were in the 1940s or even in the late 1850s, which is hard for some sportsmen to grasp in our modern day and age. However, as the red-headed stepchild of the wildfowl world, rail bird hunting is a sport which demands a light skiff, knowledge of salt marshes, and flood tides. You also need a good, strong back for poling your skiff during a good flood tide that will allow you to have an exceptional hunt.

Perhaps if rail bird hunting was easier, there might be more dove, duck, and goose hunters pursuing rail birds across North America's fresh and saltwater marshes.

Each outdoorsman will have to decide for themselves if they are interested in getting the necessary equipment, and getting out scouting their local public marshes, and then waiting for a flood tide day to go out on the marsh and trying some traditional rail bird hunting. They can also hire a professional rail bird guide for a flood tide. Either way, you will be happy you did—and will probably say to yourself, as thousands of others have thought, "Why did I wait so long to do this exceptional hunting experience?"

It is fun…great fun, and quite exceptional shooting. Every good flood tide day can provide you with just as much shooting as your most memorable opening-day dove shoot. That is a comparison many hunters can grasp to better understand just how much shooting can go on in a good rail bird hunt during a flood tide. What are you waiting for? Book a trip as soon as possible for the next available super flood tide!

Down in Florida, the best salt marshes are in the northeastern part of that state, and it's all due to the flood tides. There is some good hunting in the marshes behind Amelia Island, Florida, during a big flood tide. Years ago, when I lived in that wonderful state, there were lots of Clappers down there. I was later stationed a couple of times down on the Gulf in Tampa, Florida, and I can tell you firsthand that there are some mighty excellent duck and marsh hen hunting in the marshes off the Banana River, the Indian River lagoon, and all the way up the northeastern coastal inshore marshes to Amelia Island's salt marshes. However, you really need a skinny water boat to get at them during a high flood tide. Check with the FL-DNR for current regulations. There are lots of salt marshes on the Gulf side, and fresh water lake marshes too. However, the Gulf of Mexico has very small high tides, and you just do not have tide enough to flood the salt marshes along the Gulf of Mexico inshore marshes for traditional rail bird hunting, like you can experience along the Atlantic Coast's marshes behind the barrier islands. Do you realize that there are approximately 1.85

million acres of salt water marshes from the marshes of Maine to northeastern Florida? Look at the historical satellite photos of how much loss of Saltmarsh has occurred along the Gulf Coast just since the 1940s just due to storm damage, and you should be proud to realize just how lucky we are to have so much saltmarshes along the Atlantic Coast.

Occasionally along the coastal inshore saltmarshes in Virginia, the Carolinas, Georgia, and Florida, I'd notice various young fellows try walking up Clappers in a salt marsh during September's ties prior to a high flood tide. They never get but a handful of Clappers walking, and certainly they find it tough walking on the salt marsh, but they do get a few rail birds every September if they are knowledgeable of those areas. However, they needed to learn to do it the traditional way of poling a skiff or light boat through the salt marsh where the rail birds are found, if they are going to kill limits of rail birds consistently.

The doctor friend of mine who hunted with me one fall had to do a little bit of emergency surgery on one of those fellows, who got cut up when he fell in some green Spartina grass. That is why it's important to keep a small emergency medical kit in your boat, as you never know just when it may be needed! I believe a lot of waterfowlers have never done much rail bird hunting, as I receive a lot of phone calls from people from all over the nation who want to talk to me about hunting rail birds after reading an article I wrote, or seeing one of my rail bird hunting videos on YouTube.

Most coastal salt marshes all along the Atlantic Flyway in late September, and by October's full moon week, get loaded down with rail birds. If you really make the effort to get out there and do some serious scouting, and get to pole a salt marsh, anyone can get in some mighty excellent shot gunning for rail birds. You will find a fair amount of Soras and a lot of Clappers along the southeastern salt marshes from Maryland to Florida.

Marsh Hen (Clapper) takes flight...(Joe Guide photo)

Down in southwestern Florida, I have found quite a number of rail birds in the salt marshes along the northwest Gulf Coast of Florida, in November well above and below the Yankeetown and Homosassa salt marshes, and all around the northwestern Big Bend region marshes all the way to Mobile Bay's delta, which has in October and early November a tremendous number of rail birds. However, it appears to me when I am out there, that there are not many hunters pursuing rail birds. I do get a lot of fishermen come and talk to me after watching me hunt rail birds all over the Gulf coastal regions whenever, I am traveling and hunting through those states and researching wilderness area rail bird marshes for this book.

Even with a liberal 25-bird Sora/King rail bag limit, and 15-bird Clapper and Virginia rail bag limit per person, most Atlantic coastal states still record HIP records each year from less than 350 hunters, who state for the record that they pursue rail each season, according to the HIP data. Virtually no one I meet across the nation hunts rails to my knowledge with falconry in our day and age. However, some state Migratory Wildfowl Committees still set aside bag limits and seasons for falconry hunting in their season regulations. It is an ancient holdover of a distant time, when less than ten individuals from the wealthy élite utilized falconry to occasionally hunt migratory birds.

There is a lot of money in decoys, and You will see in this book, two beautiful carvings, one of a Clapper rail running between some Spartina grass, from carver Douglas Hiserodt of Maine, and one of a Virginia rail by Ken Sheeler of Vineland, N.J, he normally does mostly waterfowl, however he has done only five full rail bird carvings, this one with its wings outstretched, originally sold for approximately $3000 back in the 1970s. There is another rail bird a clapper rail carving from the 1980s, entitled: "Thin as a rail," by Maine decoy carving master craftsman: Doug Hiserodt. That particular carving won best in show, back in the world carving championships. It sold for $ 5,000, and it's such a lovely full body carving that is most unique, and a classic in craftsmanship for this species. A handful of other carvers that I will mention here is Jamie P. Hand from Cape May County, N.J., and Bob White and George Stunk from the state of Pennsylvania are some other excellent master decoy carvers whose wildfowl and shorebird carvings have become collector's items. Jeff Joloquett of Hampstead, N.C., is another decoy carver that I also wish to mention.

Rail bird hunting is serious business, and difficult poling, and not all God's children in the wildfowl community have shallow draft skiffs or skinny water Jon boats to adequately pursue rail birds during a proper flood tide. However, I think when more sporting gentlemen get into shooting rail birds; it will certainly grow in popularity throughout the Atlantic Flyway, where it's always been a popular hunting endeavor.

I have seen all kinds of boats and rigs when out rail bird hunting throughout the years and while hunting across the United States. Some boats are just too heavy to get back into flooded flats where more rail birds might be located, whereas a smaller and lighter flats or jon-boat or skiff would work much better. You see, it is deep within these wilderness marsh areas that Rallidae abound, and one must understand how to hunt those specific saltwater and fresh water marsh areas. Hunters also need to keep up with the migration of the rail birds in various marsh areas. That in itself takes time and effort, and is vastly important in your future planning for a good hunt when flood tides are scheduled to occur. Without strong northeast winds, you might experience 90 minutes to perhaps two hours of a good flood tide to hunt rails.

I tell people across the nation, that you cannot properly hunt rail birds with just any boat. What you need is a good light, shallow draft Jon boat or a skiff, as a deeper draft boat can be difficult to pole in many areas with heavier drafting boats or skiff salt marshes for most people. You see, it's the poling that gets to you. Try poling one or two people in an incoming high tide for a couple of hours, and you will see what I mean. Therefore, a good rail hunting guide—someone who really knows the rail bird hunting areas, and has a good light skiff, and keeps up with the rail bird migration in various local areas—is worth their weight in gold.

15 year old Chase with a limit of clapper rails on the D3 MarshMaster Skiff (Nov 2013)

Flooded rice is loaded with rail birds (Dave White Maurice River Sora rail hunt photo)

RECIPES AND COOKING

RAIL HUNTERS BIBLE Rail Birds Recipe # 1: Broiled, Baked, or Grilled?

Think about it carefully. When I think of preparing Clapper or Virginia rail as table fare, one must need, at the minimum, 4 to 8 breasts to make an average dinner meal for two to four persons.

Large people may very well ask for more helpings, and if you are a good cook, you'd better ask them before you unfreeze your rail breasts, and inquire as to how many they wish to devour. Baptists will forgo any wine, so you'd better fix a big pitcher of iced tea. Presbyterians, Episcopalians, and Roman Catholics will appreciate a good bottle of wine with any good meal. Lutherans always like a cold beer with their meal. All youngsters should drink a tall glass of milk or ice water, until they reach the age of accountability to appreciate a good glass of wine with their wild game dinner.

Sora Rail bird breasts grilled to perfection

First, a few comments regarding the accompaniment to this most excellent repast; and you will remember they will taste similar to quail. You could grill them, basting them with some special sauce you have concocted, or use a South Carolina mustard base with onions, salt, and pepper. You may wish to go wild. I like to use some Bulls Bay Sea Salt, which you can find via fine grocery stores along the South Carolina coast, or purchase from their website: www.bullsbayseasalt.com. Some friends enjoy a plethora of sea food as side dishes, such as blue crabs or shrimp-kebabs, but you think about what you desire to accompany your meal before you prepare it.

Breast your birds after your hunt, package 4 breasts per one gallon zip lock bag, and freeze the other birds, but consider carefully what other vegetables you may wish to have with your wild game meal. I caution you not to just stop there. Vegetables and rice are always nice whenever we are cooking up some rail birds for lunch or dinner. The noodle or the tender spring pea would be narcissistic to imagine that it already contains within its cell structures, all the perfection it would ever need. The chef in your kitchen may disagree with me, but that is all right. I will keep it simple.

Snow peas or lentils are nice, too. It is also important that we humans seem to fear that we are failures at being tender and springy, if we ourselves occasionally may need to be seasoned in life's great wildfowling adventures, or in preparation for the joys of feasting on outdoor game such as the noble rail bird?

I challenge the reader in this light.

If it's not so, it doesn't reflect badly on your choice of rice (dirty or sticky), or the type of pasta you may choose to accompany your meal, or the butterbean or the green pea, or the particular person that either wants or needs help in the kitchen, in order to enjoy all the good life that the Great Outdoors has to offer. Nevertheless, one must be true to oneself. You heart and your mind is to be put to good use in selecting the ingredients at the table of life. It is not so in the kitchen? Is it your kitchen, or your wife's kitchen? Permission must be acquired by the chief cook and bottle washer. "Keep the peace at all times in the kitchen," as my mama, Mrs. Martha Dinkins, would always tell her children when we were arguing over certain recipes.

THE RAIL BIRD HUNTER'S BIBLE Recipe # 2:
How to prepare and bake a Sora PEEP PIE.

How do you bake a Sora pie, Billy Boy, Billy Boy? My cousin Billy Threat gave me this recipe for a Sora rail Peep Pie. You will need a baking pan, flour, and baking and rolling utensils, if you wish to roll out your own dough. Perhaps you may desire to obtain an already layered pie pan, the size you would use to make homemade chicken pot pie, if that floats your boat. My wife doesn't let me cook that often in her kitchen, so I like to flour and roll my own dough for the pie pan from scratch, but I am kind of old school about these things and take enjoyment from them, and my friends enjoy it immensely.

Dice up half a peeled potato, add a handful of diced carrots and peas, and I always enjoy adding a small onion, diced up well. Spices are nice, depending on your own taste.

I'll use four to six Sora rail breasts that have been soaking overnight in a mixture of Teriyaki, salt and pepper, and a little bit of good red wine, all mixed and placed with the breasts inside a Tupperware sealed bowl. You can also wrap a small piece of pre-cooked bacon around each breast while marinating, secured with a colored toothpick.

Preheat your oven to 350 degrees, and then bake your pie for approximately 35 minutes. Check your pies to ensure uniformity in baking, and that each Peep Pie is ready for the dinner table. To enjoy this meal, have a side dish of sticky or wild rice, and perhaps some fried okra.

I wash all this down with a nice bottle of Merlot, or perhaps a exceptional bottle of Australian Red Wine (Penfold Coonawarra Bin 128 or Bin 58) from the Adele region of South Australia, which is another favorite of mine. I enjoy sharing a good bottle of wine with friends when we have dinner such as this in order to accompany the wild game meal.

I am just a low country cook, and try to enjoy cooking for my friends. I will offer in this chapter on cooking a few major and tasty meals for you to try after your next rail hunt.

THE RAIL BIRD HUNTERS BIBLE Recipe #3:
Rail Bird Bites
(Recipe from Darryl Bogart of New Jersey)

Sora breasts should be marinated prior to your meal, and placed in a Tupperware bowl in the fridge. Prior to grilling the breasts, add seasoning, salt, and pepper. Author's note: My wife likes to marinate Sora breasts in a combination of Teriyaki with lemon, salt and pepper, but please don't overdo the spices. Grill to perfection; serve with a seafood dish on the side.

THE RAIL BIRD HUNTERS BIBLE Recipe # 4:
Rail Bird Luncheon

Get a bunch of rail bird breasts out of the freezer. Depending on the numbers you have over for lunch, the average recommendation is four breasts per person.

Grill the Sora rail bird bosoms until they are nice, tender and juicy. As they have been feasting on rice, you will learn to savor them when prepared in this manner. Prepare and serve to your guests with toothpicks on a serving tray as *hors d'oeuvres* and as part of your pre-dinner meal, prior to the main course of salad, corn on the cob, green beans, and the main course of seafood—scallops, and a good ol' shrimp boil.

Ya'll can wash it all down with a good bottle of red wine from Trueluck Vineyards (Florence, S.C), or perhaps one from Duplin Wines near Pink Hill, N.C. Your wife might just tell you to head over to the local Harris Teeter's, or Food Lion grocery store and grab a bottle of Yellow Tail, of course you've serve ice water/sweet tea for the youngsters, and give everyone that behaved themselves throughout the meal a nice slice of Key Lime Pie, or Mrs. Smith's pecan pie for dessert. Man, that good southern eating…it's good in the Carolinas, or even in South Maine or South Jersey! You will never say, "Where's the beef?" after you've munched down on some tasty rail bird breasts.

ABOUT THE AUTHOR

U.S. Navy Commander Walter Dinkins, USNR (Ret), writes under the name "Joe Guide," and he operates **JOE GUIDE OUTFITTERS,** based out of the port city of Wilmington, North Carolina, in the southeastern part of the state, where he resides with his family. You can visit his website: at www.joeguideoutfitters.com.

He has been rail bird hunting since he was just a young fellow, and that first hunt was in October of 1968. He grew up in the low country of South Carolina, where his grandmother' family, owned three farms in three counties from the 1680s–1980s. He retired from the U.S. Navy Chaplain Corps after 30 years and one month of honorable service, and deployed into five combat zones during his many years of service in the U.S. Armed Forces. He served with U.S. Marines FMF commands, U.S. Navy Ships and Shore assignments, Combatant Commands, the USCG in Alaska and the Keys, and USA Commands, and he even covered USAF detachments during joint service command assignments. His work has taken him all over the world, and back again to the Carolina coast. He enjoys guiding saltwater fly fishermen in the spring and summer months, and wildfowlers throughout the rail bird seasons of the year. In the winter months, he's busy guiding waterfowl hunters.

CDR Walter Dinkins, CHC USN SEAL Team Two Chaplain Towin Kowt Afghanistan-April 2012

When not on the water or traveling, he continues his work with *Wounded Warrior Programs*, and volunteers with organizations such as the veterans' hospitals and Project

Healing Waters Fly Fishing (PHWFF) as the "Chaplain for the Deep South Region." He enjoys taking out a limited number of Wounded Warriors fly fishing and wildfowl hunting during the seasons of the year. He is a Presbyterian minister and chaplain, and you can Google him to see videos of him preaching and talking at various cities, communities, and military bases around the nation and the world.

Chaplain W. Dinkins USNR BUMED. Nov 2011 Wounded Warrior Surfing program Del Mar Beach, CA.

He is often invited to lecture on ethics and military history, and perhaps you can hear him speak or preach somewhere near your hometown, or somewhere across our nation. He currently serves on the Ethics Committee for the Outdoor Writers Association of America (OWAA), and is a member of the Southern Order of Storytellers.

If you desire to book a rail bird hunt with Joe Guide Outfitters, please book early, as there are a limited number of super flood tides during the rail bird hunting season. Some months there may be just six or eight days during each month of rail bird season. You can book him via the **JOE GUIDE OUTFITTERS** website, which is noted in the first paragraph of this section.

Author at work in a Medical Humanitarian Mission Refugee Camp: Djibouti, Africa, January 2008

Skinny as a Railbird. Carving by Doug Hiserodt

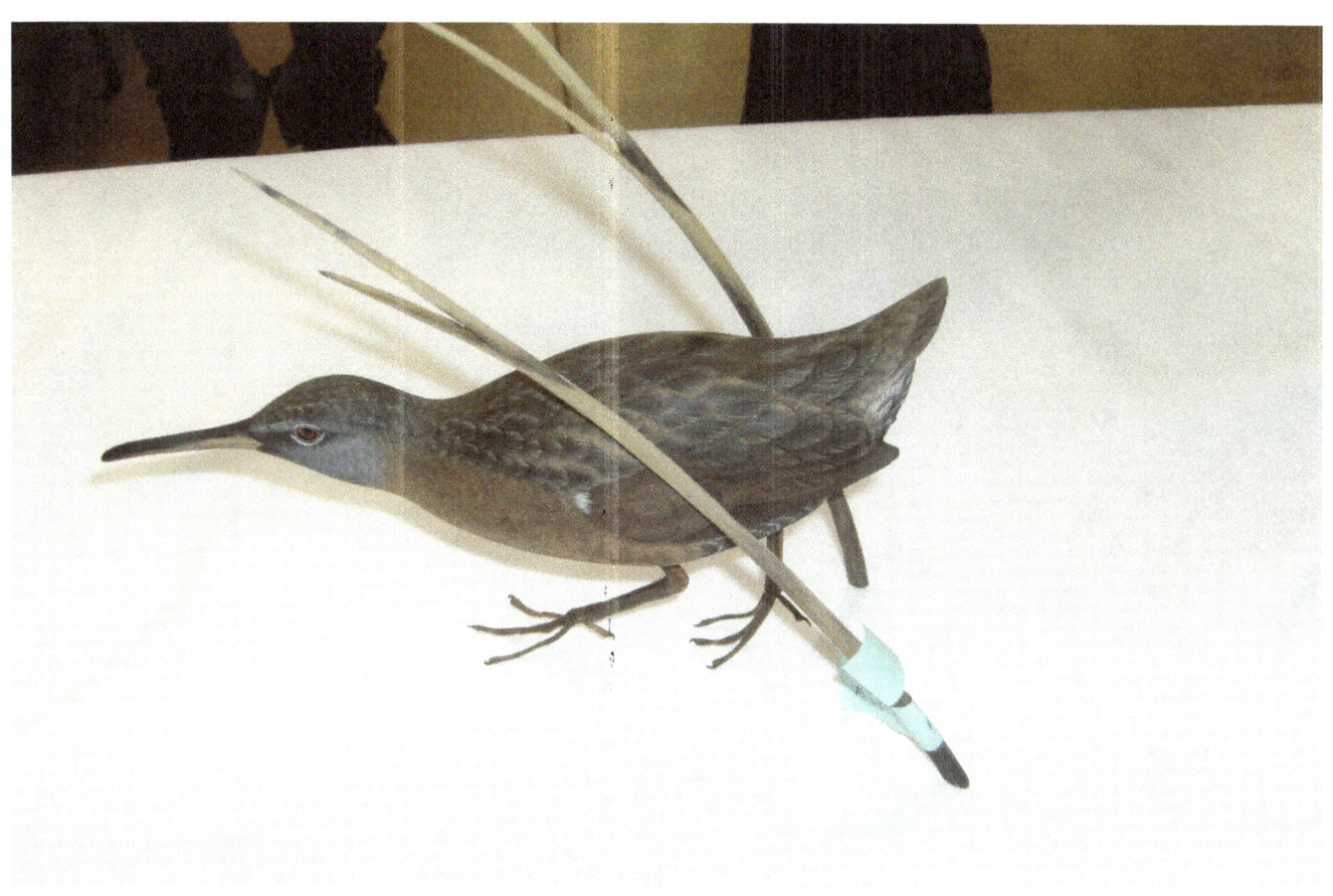

Doug Hiserodt's award winning-rail bird carving

BIBLIOGRAPHY & SCHOLARLY SOURCES

Allen, E G., 1951 History of American Ornithology before Audubon. Transcript of the lecture before the American Philosophical Society 41:387-591.

Andrews, D. A. 1973. *Habitat utilization by Sora, Virginia Rails, and King Rails near Southwestern Lake Erie*. Master of Science Thesis; Ohio State University.

Audubon, John J. 1843 *Journal of Field Notes* complied from his *Research on Rail Bird Species, and his 1811-1814 Personal Journal of his visits throughout the Atlantic Coastal States and the Mississippi Valley* IRT: Southern States Wildfowl Studies.

Bateman, H.A., Jr. 1977. King Rail. Pages 93-104 in: Sanderson, G. C. [Ed.] Management of Migratory shore and upland game birds in North America. University of Nebraska Press.

Bogart, D., Nov 2013; and J.P. Hand. Dec 2013 Interview with Dinkins, Walter M., "Lessons learned from Thirty + years of hunting rail birds on the Maurice River's Rice Meadows, N.J.

Bogardus, Adam H. Field, *Cover and Trap Shooting*. New York: J.B. Ford 1874. Bauer, Eddie. *The Waterfowlers Bible*.

Conway, C.J. 1990. Seasonal changes in movements and habitat use by species of rails. M.S. Thesis, University of Wyoming, Laramie, WY.

Cooper T.R. (Ed.). 2006, King Rail conservation action plan workshop summary: 14-15 November 2006, Memphis, TN. Unpublished report.

Craig, R. J. 1990. *Historic trends in the distribution and population of estuarine marsh birds of the Connecticut River*. Research Report #83. Department of Natural Resources Management and Engineering, College of Agriculture and Natural Resources. U.CONN.

Dodd, M.G., T.M. Murphy, D.C. Hahn, and R.L. Joyner. 1999. Managing brackish coastal wetlands for increased biological diversity and abundance. Technical Report to S.C. Division of Natural resources, Columbia, SC.

Dinkins, W.M. *Rail bird hunting and Research Journal notes*: "*Rail Bird Hunting across the USA. 1968-Present, Personal Journal.*

Eddleman. W.R., and C.J. Conway. 1994. (Pages 168-179 in *Migratory Shore and Upland Game Bird Management in North America* (T.C. Tacha and C.E. Braun, Eds.). The International Association of Fish and Wildlife Agencies, Lawrence, KS.

Eddleman, W.R., F.L. Knopf, B. Meanley, F.A. Reid, and R. Zembal. 1988. Conservation of North American Rallids. Wilson Bulletin 100:458-475.

Gaines, K.F., J.C. Cumbee, and W.L. Stevens. 2003. Nest characteristics of the Clapper Rail in coastal Georgia. Journal of Field Ornithology 74:152-156.

Gauthier, G. 1988. Territorial behavior, forced copulations, and mixed reproductive strategy. WILDFOWL 39"102-114.

Gordon, D.H.,B.T. Gray, R.D. Perry, M.B. Prevost, T.H. Strange, and R. K. Williams, 1989. South Atlantic Coastal Wetlands. Pages 57-92 in L.M. Smith, R.L. Pederson, and R. M. Kaminski, editors. Habitat management for migrating and wintering waterfowl in North America. Texas Tech University Press, Lubbock, TX.

Graves, C.A. 2001. Avian use of tidal marshes across a salinity gradient at Savannah National Wildlife Refuge, Georgia-South Carolina. M.S. thesis, University of Tennessee, Knoxville, TN.

Gresham, Grits. *The Complete Wildfowler*.1975. Page 24-26. Follett Publishing Company.

Lewis, Elisha J. *The American Sportsman*. New York: Lippincott, 1857.

Lewis, J.C., and R.L. Garrison. 1983. Habitat suitability index models: Clapper Rails in managed impoundments, and tidal marshes. M.S. thesis, University of Georgia, Athens, GA.

Long, Joseph W. American Wildfowl Shooting. New York: Orange, Judd, 1879.

Mackey, William J. *American Bird Decoys*. New York: E.P. Dutton, 1965.

Manci, K. M. and D. H. Rusch. 1988. *Indices to distribution and abundance of some inconspicuous water birds of Horicon Marsh*. Journal of Field Ornithology Pages: 67-75

McClintock, C.P., T.C. Williams, and J.M. Teal. 1978. Autumn Bird Migrations Observed from Ships in the Western Atlantic Ocean. Wilson Ornithological Bulletin 49:262-277.

Meanley, B. 1953. Nesting of the King Rail in the Arkansas rice fields. Pages 262-269.

Meanley, B. 1957. Notes on the courtship behavior of the King Rail. Pages: 433-440.

Meanley, B. 1969. Natural history of the King Rail. North American Fauna No. 67.

Meanley, B. 1985. The Marsh Hen. Centreville, Maryland. Tidewater Publishers.

Meanley, B. *and* D. K. Wetherbee. 1962. *Ecological notes on mixed populations of King Rails and Clapper Rails in the Delaware Bay marshes.*

Odom, Ron R., Mercury Contamination in Georgia Rails. GA-DNR-Game and Fish Division. October 1971 and September 1973 Field Studies.

Perkins, M. 2007. The use of stable isotopes to determine the ratio of resident to migrant king rails in southern Louisiana and Texas. MS Thesis, Louisiana State University.

Peterson, Roger Tory. A Field Guide to the Birds, Volume 1. Houghton Mifflin, 1947.

Pierluissi, S. 2006. Breeding Water Birds use of Rice Fields in Southwestern Louisiana. MS Thesis, Louisiana State University.

Pospichal, L. B. and W. H. Marshall. 1954. A field study of the Sora Rail and Virginia Rail in central Minnesota. Flicker 26:2-32.

Porteus, Frank. Interview: Nov 15 2010, and Dec 28, 2011 with author: *"Hunting rail birds along the Connecticut River's Great Rice Meadows in the 1950s and 1960s below Essex, CN."*

Price, Iola. The Effects of toxic chemicals on Colonial freshwater and marine water birds, as well as the relationship between their groups, and aquaculture. University of Ontario, Canada. M.Sc., Thesis.

Rappole, J. H., and A.R. Tipton. 1991. New harness design for attachment of radio transmitters to small passerines. Journal of Field Ornithology 62:335-337.

Reid, F. A. 1989. *Differential Habitat Use by Water birds in a Managed Wetland* Complex. PhD Dissertation, University of Missouri – Columbia.

Reiger, George 1989. The Wildfowlers Quest. Lyons & Burford Publishers, NY.

Rundle, W.D., and L.H. Fredrickson. 1981. Managing seasonally flooded impoundments for migrant rails and shorebirds. Wildlife Society Bulletin 9:80-86. Society of Canadian Ornithologist's (Societe' des Ornithologists du Canada).

Sprunt, A., IV, and Zim, H.S. *Game Birds*. New York: Golden Press, 1961.

Stone, J.H. III., *Interview rail bird hunting-Beaufort, and Charleston, S.C.* 2004.

TACHA, R. W. 1975. A survey of rail populations in Kansas, with emphasis on the Cheyenne Bottoms. M.S. thesis, Fort Hays Kansas State Coll., Hays, Kansas.

Tanner, W.D., and G.O. Hendrickson. 1954. Ecology of the Virginia Rail in Clay County, Iowa. Iowa Bird Life 24:65-70.

Tomlinson, R.E., and R.L. Todd. 1973. Distribution of two western Clapper Rail races as determined by responses to taped calls. Condor 75:177-183 USDFW.

Tanner, W. D. 1953. Ecology of the Virginia and King Rails and the Sora in Clay County, Iowa. PhD Dissertation, Iowa State College.

Tori, G.M., S.Mcleod, K. Mcknight, T. Moorman, and F.A. Reid. 2002. Wetland conservation, and Ducks Unlimited: real world approaches to multispecies management. Waterbirds 25:115-121. Wilson Journal of Ornithology

Weiss, R. A. 1995. The Status and Distribution of Rails, and Other Marsh Birds in Natural and Restored Wetlands in Indiana. PhD Dissertation; Ball State University, Indiana.

Wolters, Richard A. *Water Dog*. New York: E.P. Dutton. 1964.

Zembal, R., B.W. Massey, and J.M. Fancher. 1989. Movement and activity patterns of the Light-footed Clapper Rail. Journal of Wildlife Management 53:39-42

Author with Professor Joe who limited out in 21 shots. 31 Oct 2011

www.ingramcontent.com/pod-product-compliance
Lightning Source LLC
Chambersburg PA
CBHW082124230426
43671CB00015B/2798